ARGENTINA
in Pictures

VGS

Tom Streissguth

Lerner Publications Company

Contents

Lerner Publishing Group realizes that current information and statistics quickly become out of date. To extend the usefulness of the Visual Geography Series, we developed www.vgsbooks.com, a website offering links to up-to-date information, as well as in-depth material, on a wide variety of subjects. All of the websites listed on www.vgsbooks.com have been carefully selected by researchers at Lerner Publishing Group. However, Lerner Publishing Group is not responsible for the accuracy or suitability of the material on any website other than <www.lernerbooks.com>. It is recommended that students using the Internet be supervised by a parent or teacher. Links on www.vgsbooks.com will be regularly reviewed and updated as needed.

INTRODUCTION   4

THE LAND   8

▶ Regions. Flora and Fauna. Climate. Natural Resources. Rivers. Cities.

HISTORY AND GOVERNMENT   20

▶ Exploration and Settlement. The Viceroyalty. The Fight for Independence. Political Turmoil. Immigration and Prosperity. The Era of Perón. Military Rule. Amnesty and Economics. Government.

THE PEOPLE   36

▶ Ethnic Heritage and Language. Religion. Health and Social Welfare. Education.

Lerner Publications Company
A division of Lerner Publishing Group
241 First Avenue North
Minneapolis, MN 55401 U.S.A.

Website address: www.lernerbooks.com

web enhanced @ www.vgsbooks.com

CULTURAL LIFE   46

► Holidays and Celebrations. Music. Literature and Art. Sports. Food.

THE ECONOMY   56

► Manufacturing. Farming and Forestry. Mining and Energy. Services. Mercosur and Foreign Trade. The Future.

FOR MORE INFORMATION

► Timeline	66
► Fast Facts	68
► Currency	68
► Flag	69
► National Anthem	69
► Famous People	70
► Sights to See	72
► Glossary	73
► Selected Bibliography	74
► Further Reading and Websites	76
► Index	78

Library of Congress Cataloging-in-Publication Data

Streissguth, Tom, 1958–
    Argentina in pictures / by Tom Streissguth.—Rev. & expanded.
       p.   cm. — (Visual geography series)
    Includes bibliographical references and index.
    ISBN: 0-8225-0372-7 (lib. bdg. : alk. paper)
    1. Argentina—Juvenile literature. I. Title. II. Visual geography series (Minneapolis, Minn.)
F2808.2 .S76 2003
982—dc21
                                            2002004713

Manufactured in the United States of America
1 2 3 4 5 6 - JR - 08 07 06 05 04 03

INTRODUCTION

Stretching from the tropics almost to the continent of Antarctica, the Argentine Republic boasts a varied landscape of towering mountains, deep forests, humid lowlands, and flat, fertile plains. Forming the southeastern quarter of South America, Argentina lies behind imposing geographical barriers, including the Andes Mountains and the Amazonian tropical forests, that have cut it off from the rest of the continent. Culturally, Argentines also feel distinct and separate from the rest of Latin America. With a national heritage of immigrants from Spain and many other countries, they live among a diversity of nationalities that, at one time, lent the country a sense of future possibility and opportunity.

But for more than two hundred years after the first arrival of Europeans, Argentina was a backwater of South American colonization, a remote and neglected region where settlers found that mere survival was a challenge. After the nation gained its independence from Spain in the early nineteenth century, Argentines endured many

decades of leadership conflicts, as two opposing factions, known as the *federales* and *unitarios*, fought for power over the nation's political and economic institutions. But, even as dictatorships rose and fell, the country's resources and prosperity attracted immigrants from around the world.

A key component of the nation's wealth was its vast expanse of fertile land for raising crops and grazing cattle. The nation's farmers and livestock herders made up a vital economic foundation upon which modern industries developed through the first half of the twentieth century. While the economy grew, a vibrant cultural scene thrived in the capital of Buenos Aires, where artists, writers, musicians, and filmmakers prospered. Argentina built a strong educational system and produced leading scientists in many fields. Although they were often sharply divided on political issues, Argentines also considered themselves to be citizens of one of the world's most civilized nations.

Nevertheless, political instability has plagued Argentina throughout its modern history. In the mid-twentieth century, President Juan Perón and his wife Eva were prominent political leaders who gained a great following. But even Perón lost popularity. The coup d'état (the sudden, often violent, overthrow of a government) became almost a commonplace event, as army leaders forced their way into power. Like many other former European colonies in South America, the country struggled to establish a stable, democratic government.

Severe economic problems have also had damaging effects. During some periods in the twentieth century, Argentina was one of the fastest-growing nations in the world, while during others it was an economic disaster area. Hyperinflation—a rapid and steep decline in the value of the national currency combined with rising prices—destroyed the savings and livelihoods of many Argentines in the 1970s and 1980s. Political leaders undertook sweeping reforms to improve the nation's economy—and failed. High amounts of government spending and large debts to other nations drained Argentina's treasury and discouraged foreign investors.

After the beginnings of a slow recovery in the 1990s, the first years of the twenty-first century brought economic crisis yet again. After several years of stable prices, inflation took hold once more. In late 2001, Argentina failed to make payments on its debts to foreign lenders. The country's currency lost value, and, when the government declared bank accounts frozen, many Argentines watched helplessly as their life savings vanished. Riots and turmoil swept through Argentine cities in late 2001 and into 2002, while a series of interim presidents found themselves unable to solve the chronic problems brought by years of failed policies. Although Argentina benefits from a wealth of resources and a modernized industrial sector, the country still faces very tough problems that defy easy solutions.

THE LAND

The Argentine Republic covers nearly 1.1 million square miles (2.8 million square kilometers) of southeastern South America. The eighth largest country in the world, Argentina stretches 2,175 miles (3,500 km) from north to south and 870 miles (1,400 km) from east to west at its widest point. The country's 3,200-mile (5,150-km) western border meets Chile along the long, high chain of the Andes Mountains. To the northwest lies Bolivia, and in the north is Paraguay. Argentina's northeastern neighbors are Brazil and Uruguay. The seacoast of eastern Argentina runs for 3,100 miles (4,989 km) along the Atlantic Ocean, from the estuary of the Río de la Plata in the north to Tierra del Fuego in the south.

Argentina also claims South Georgia Island, the South Sandwich Islands, and a pie-shaped wedge of Antarctica that covers 463,321 square miles (1.2 million sq. km). The Falkland Islands, known to Argentines as the Islas Malvinas, belong to Britain, although Argentina tried unsuccessfully to take over the islands in 1982.

▶ Regions

Mesopotamia, a region in northeastern Argentina whose name means "between the rivers," lies between the Río Paraná and Río Uruguay. Plentiful rainfall nourishes the network of rivers and streams that flow through this low-lying and marshy land. Sheep, horse, and cattle raising are common livelihoods in southern Mesopotamia. Along the border with Brazil, Iguazú Falls tumbles over a series of cascades dropping 269 feet (82 meters) into the Río Iguazú.

The Chaco region of tropical rain forests and drier savanna (grassland with few trees) covers north central Argentina. The Chaco, which means "hunting ground," forms the southern portion of South America's larger Gran Chaco, which stretches into Bolivia and Paraguay. Between the Chaco region and the Andes Mountains to the west rises the altiplano, a high, dry plateau. The puna, an arid, desert-like region, runs from the province of Catamarca to Bolivia, also crossing the border with Chile.

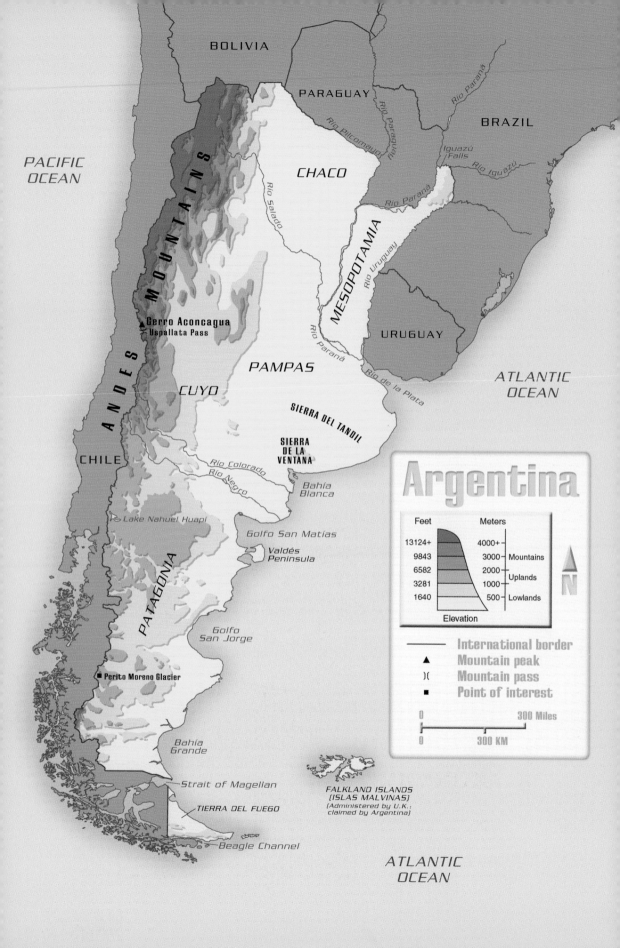

The pampas of central Argentina stretches 600 miles (966 km) west and south of Buenos Aires. A region of flat, fertile plains and grasslands, the pampas is the country's most productive agricultural region. This "breadbasket" provides grain, beef, and other valuable products and exports.

The pampas is divided into the *pampa húmeda* to the east and the *pampa seca* to the west. The pampa húmeda, or "humid pampas," is a fertile region for growing grain and herding livestock. The pampa seca, or "dry pampas," is a drier, less populated area that is home to a variety of scrub plants and grass but that has few trees except those planted to serve as windbreaks. Low ranges, including the Sierra del Tandil and the Sierra de la Ventana to the east, break the level landscape.

The desertlike Cuyo region in west central Argentina includes San Juan, Mendoza, and San Luis Provinces. The Andes Mountains tower to the west, reaching 22,834 feet (6,960 m) above sea level at Cerro Aconcagua, the highest point in the Western Hemisphere. Wide gulches known as *quebradas* separate the peaks of the Andes, providing transportation routes to western South America. Just south of Cerro Aconcagua lies the Uspallata Pass, where the Pan-American Highway links Argentina and Chile. Overlooking the pass is the Cristo Redentor, or Christ of the Andes statue, built in 1904 to mark Argentina and Chile's final agreement on the boundary between them.

Teams of paleontologists have found hundreds of dinosaur fossils in the arid **Valle de la Luna** (Moon Valley) in San Juan Province. Many of these fossils are of species that had been previously unknown to science.

The **Perito Moreno glacier** averages 2.5 miles (4 km) wide and 192 feet (60 m) high.

Patagonia covers about one-quarter of Argentina, beginning at the Río Colorado in the north. Glaciers cover the higher mountain slopes to the west. The huge Perito Moreno glacier descends to Lago Argentino where, about once every three years, melting waters burst through the glacier's face and rush into the lake. Deep canyons criss-cross Patagonia, where rock formations tower over rugged, windswept plains. In the early twentieth century, irrigation canals were built to divert water from the Río Negro to help farmers working in this dry, windswept region.

In east central Patagonia lies the Valdés Peninsula, which juts into the Atlantic Ocean on the southern rim of the Golfo San Matías. The peninsula claims the lowest elevation in Argentina at 131 feet (40 m) below sea level. At the southern tip of Argentina, the Strait of Magellan and the Beagle Channel flow past Tierra del Fuego, the "Land of Fire." Argentina and Chile each own a portion of this cold, windy territory, named by European sailors for the campfires lit by indigenous people onshore.

Farther to the south, Argentina has long claimed a small portion of Antarctica as its national territory. Other nations, including the United States, have disputed these claims. Despite these disagreements, Argentina operates year-round research stations on Antarctica. It has also been a party to the Antarctic Treaty, the Convention for the Conservation of Antarctic Seals, and the Convention on the Conservation of Antarctic Marine Living Resources.

Flora and Fauna

The plant life of Argentina varies greatly with latitude and with elevation. In the south, thorny shrubs and lichens thrive in the mountain valleys, and beech forests grow in areas of heavy rainfall. To the north, much of the grassy pampas has no native tree growth at all. Argentines divide the dominant flora of the pampas into *pasto duro* (hard grass), which is edible for horses and adult cattle, and *pasto tierno* (soft grass), which is better for sheep. The tall, woolly pampas grass grows only in the southern reaches of the pampas.

On the lower slopes of the Andes, the most common trees are oak, cedar, pine, and laurel. The tropical Gran Chaco region holds abundant hardwood trees, including the quebracho, algaroba, *palosanto*, and *lapacho*. A variety of plants native to Europe have also been imported and cultivated, including barley, wheat, alfalfa, and many different fruit trees, as well as the Australian eucalyptus.

Argentina's native animals have suffered with the settlement and cultivation of the land. Tapirs, peccaries, monkeys, martens, and pumas live in the Chaco and the tropical forests of the north. The

Argentina's **beech forests** are prized by environmentalists as well as by multinational timber and paper corporations.

The fleece of the **alpaca** comes in more than twenty natural colors, and it is often preferred to sheep's wool for making clothing. Argentine alpaca are raised for this purpose and sheared annually.

habitat of the guanaco and alpaca, animals similar to the llama, stretches nearly the entire length of Argentina. On the pampas, the cattle herds brought by European settlers have attracted new predators such as the puma and the jaguar. The viscacha, a small animal related to the chinchilla, lives in large colonies on the pampas, a place with little natural shelter and where few large species make their homes. Foxes, hares, armadillos, wolves, small wildcats, and seals live in Patagonia. Along the coast, immense flocks of gulls and other seabirds nest along river estuaries and lagoons and on the rocky offshore islands. Condors, vultures, and hawks prefer the western foothills and the mountain solitude of the Andes, while the ostrichlike rhea makes its home in central Argentina and a variety of penguin species populate Patagonia and Tierra del Fuego.

The male **rhea** builds a nest and sits on the eggs, which have often been laid by more than one female, until the eggs hatch. The youngsters stay with the male for only six months but may stay with their brood for up to three years.

Climate

Most of Argentina lies in a temperate zone, with a narrow tropical area in the north and a cooler region in the south. Because Argentina lies in the Southern Hemisphere, its seasons are the reverse of those in the Northern Hemisphere. Argentina's warm summer season falls between December and March, and it has cool winter weather between June and September. The Chaco region is hot, and Cuyo stays dry and sunny through much of the year. Milder temperatures prevail in the pampas, while Patagonia and the Andes Mountains remain cool throughout the year.

Rainfall is heaviest in the north and northeast, a zone of high temperatures and high humidity. Windy rainstorms move eastward in the pampas, flooding the plains. Hot winds known as *zondas* blow on these plains, creating occasional dust storms. The heavy rains in the Chaco region cause flooding in the summer.

The high Andes Mountains along Argentina's western border have an important influence on the country's climate. The mountains prevent rain-bearing clouds from moving inland from the Pacific Ocean, keeping western Argentina dry. On the Atlantic coast, cold ocean currents often cause heavy fog and sudden drops in temperature. A strong southeast wind known as the *sudestada* occasionally blows through Patagonia and the pampas, bringing heavy rain and flash floods.

In Patagonia, rain falls throughout the year, as the Andes are lower in the south and allow rain clouds to pass more easily to the east. In the mountains, long, harsh winters are the rule. The snow line lies at 20,000 feet (6,096 m) in the warmer northwest but descends all the way down to 1,500 feet (457 m) in chilly southern Patagonia.

Natural Resources

Argentina was named by Spanish explorers after *argentum*, the Latin word for silver. Unfortunately for the Spanish, only small silver deposits exist within this country. However, Argentina does have a great swath of fertile soil in the pampas region, where the soft earth allows plants to send their roots deep underground. The volcanic red soil of northeast Argentina is also fertile and well drained.

The Cuyo region includes copper, lead, and uranium ores as well as deposits of oil and natural gas. The quebracho tree, which grows in the Chaco region, produces a hardwood used for making telephone poles, railroad ties, and fence posts. The quebracho is also a source of tannin, a resin used in the country's busy leather industry.

The yerba maté tree grows in the forests of northern Argentina and on plantations in Misiones, Corrientes, and Chaco Provinces. The leaves of the tree are dried and roasted, then boiled to make a refreshing drink, which was first concocted by the Guarani Indians.

Rivers

The Río de la Plata (River of Silver) divides Argentina and the southern part of Uruguay. Fed by several important tributaries, including the Río Uruguay and the Río Paraná, the Río de la Plata is more of an estuary than a river, forming a wide and deep basin that serves as an essential highway for commercial ships.

In the north, the Río Pilcomayo and the Río Paraguay mark Argentina's border with Paraguay. The Paraná rises in southern Brazil, passes through Iguazú National Park at the northern tip of Misiones Province in Argentina, and runs due south after reaching Corrientes and Resistencia, two provincial capitals. The Río Uruguay defines Argentina's border with Uruguay and Brazil.

A long series of east-running tributaries flows from the Andes into the pampas and Patagonia. The Río Salado, which forms the frontier

The Iguazú Falls along the Río Paraná thunder across more than two hundred separate cascades into a vast chasm along Argentina's border with Brazil. At their highest point, the falls plunge down a vertical drop that is one and a half times the full height of Niagara Falls.

between the mountain foothills and the plains, meets the 530-mile (853-km) Río Colorado in the southern pampas. Not far to the south, the Río Negro, in northern Patagonia, empties into the northern reaches of Golfo San Matías. The coast also forms Bahía Grande in southern Patagonia, Golfo San Jorge to the north, and Bahía Blanca at the southern limit of the pampas.

Cities

Buenos Aires is Argentina's capital and its largest city. Lying on the western bank of the Río de la Plata, the city's greater metropolitan area is home to more than 11 million people—nearly one-third of the country's population.

The main streets of Buenos Aires include the Avenida Nueve de Julio (Ninth of July Avenue), the widest street in the world. Calle Florida (Florida Street) offers elegant shops as well as art galleries and restaurants. Immigrants once filled the alleys of La Boca, a colorful suburb that hosts a lively artist colony. At one end of a huge square known as the Plaza de Mayo, the ornate Casa Rosada (Pink House) holds the offices of the national government and a giant maze of halls, stairways, and offices. The Catedral Metropolitana serves as a place of worship and also as a national shrine to the Argentine independence movement. Opera, concert, and ballet performances entertain audiences at the Teatro Colón.

In 1996 Madonna fans watched her sing "Don't Cry For Me, Argentina" from the balcony of the Casa Rosada, a government building in Buenos Aires. The song was part of *Evita*, a movie musical about the Argentine first lady, Eva Perón.

Buildings painted in bright, contrasting colors make La Boca a distinctive neighborhood in Buenos Aires.

Visit vgsbooks.com for links to websites featuring photos of Argentina's regional landscapes, up-to-date population figures, and current weather conditions.

Founded in the sixteenth century, Buenos Aires began as a fortification called Puerto de Nuestra Señora de Santa María del Buen Aire, or Port of Our Lady Saint Mary of the Fair Winds. It has been the scene of nearly every major political event in Argentine history. Since the eighteenth century, immigration from Argentina's own countryside and from Europe has swelled the city's population. In the early twenty-first century, Buenos Aires still feels the tension between working-class families from the country and town dwellers, who have historically held greater privileges, access to education, and political power.

The second-largest city of Argentina, Córdoba (population 1.2 million) is one of the oldest continuously inhabited places in the Americas. Córdoba lies in northwestern Argentina about 400 miles (644 km) from Buenos Aires.

Founded by Spanish explorers in 1573, Córdoba occupied a strategic position between the Andes Mountains and the plains of the pampas. It served as an economic and political center for more than two centuries, even rivaling the influence of the coastal city of Buenos Aires. The first university in Argentina was founded in Córdoba in 1613. Many historic

Argentina's first university, Universidad Nacional de Córdoba (National University of Córdoba) was a Jesuit seminary that opened in 1613. It officially became a university in 1622, making it one of the oldest in the Western Hemisphere. Harvard University in the United States was founded in 1636.

structures from the colonial period have been preserved, including the seventeenth century Iglesia Catedral and an elaborate market.

Rosario (population nearly 1 million) lies northwest of Buenos Aires in the province of Santa Fe. Located in a productive agricultural region, Rosario serves as one of the country's industrial and business hubs. Linked by the Río Paraná to the Río de la Plata, Rosario merchants and manufacturers can ship goods to the Atlantic coast, while highways leading westward provide a route for commercial traffic all the way to the Pacific coast.

Ushuaia (population 30,000) is the provincial capital of Tierra del Fuego. Lying on the Beagle Channel at the tip of Argentina, Ushuaia proudly claims the title of southernmost city in the world. A duty-free zone in Tierra del Fuego, the island of which Ushuaia is the capital, attracts trade as well as tourists to the city and its harbor. Ushuaia also serves as a jumping-off point for expeditions to Antarctica and for tourists on their way to the Tierra del Fuego National Park.

Ushuaia is 1,974 miles (3,718 km) from Buenos Aires but only 745 miles (1,200 km) from Antarctica.

HISTORY AND GOVERNMENT

Historians do not know very many details about Argentina's ancient history, but they believe that people have been living in the area for thousands of years. Artifacts such as cave paintings, pottery, and tools of stone and shell remain to give important hints about Argentina's past. From these clues, historians know that in Argentina and throughout southern South America, many tribes of indigenous peoples formed settled communities or moved from place to place in search of productive land and good hunting grounds.

To the north of Argentina, in what would become Peru, Chile, Bolivia, and Ecuador, the powerful Incan Empire thrived during the A.D. 1300s and into the early 1400s. The Incas conquered many native South American groups and controlled a large area. However, tribes such as the Diaguita of northern and western Argentina resisted the expansion of the Incan Empire into Argentina, and most of the region's indigenous groups remained independent. Other groups in northern Argentina included the Kollas (also called the Quechua), the Huarpe, and the Aymara. Some of these tribes were primarily farming groups who raised crops such as maize, pumpkin, and beans, and lived in permanent villages. Agricultural communities included the Comechingon and the Guarani in north central Argentina.

Other groups were nomadic hunters and gatherers, roaming the central and southern plains in search of wild game. Groups such as the Puelche and the Tehuelche hunted the guanaco and the rhea using long, sharp lances and the *boleadora*. The boleadora was a very effective weapon made up of two or three ropes, each with a heavy stone at the end. The hunter could fling the boleadora a long distance, bringing an animal down either by striking it with the stones or by tangling its legs in the ropes. In Patagonia, native inhabitants hunted seal and alpaca, while coastal peoples lived on fish and bird eggs.

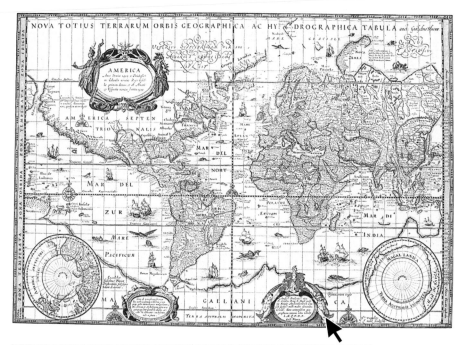

Ships and sea monsters often embellish maps such as this one from the era of the exploration and settlement of the Western Hemisphere.

Exploration and Settlement

In the late fifteenth and early sixteenth centuries, Spain and other European nations sent a series of expeditions to the Western Hemisphere. The Europeans were searching for a new trade route to the East Indies. If discovered, this route would speed up the voyage to the Asian markets that provided spices, gold, and other valuable goods for trading.

The first European explorers to see Argentina's coast arrived in 1516, during the expedition of Juan Díaz de Solís. This captain, who sailed as far south as the Río de la Plata estuary, came in search of silver, gold, and other precious resources. Finding the land around the river's mouth unpromising, Díaz de Solís sailed upstream. Soon after landing, however, his expedition was attacked by local inhabitants, and Díaz de Solís was killed. The surviving members of his crew soon returned to Spain, bringing accounts of the new land.

Ferdinand Magellan, a Portuguese voyager, sailed the length of South America's Atlantic coast and reached Tierra del Fuego in 1520. A few years later, Sebastian Cabot sailed up the Río de la Plata and explored the Río Paraguay and the Río Paraná.

Ferdinand Magellan

During this expedition, Cabot founded Sancti Spiritus, the first Spanish settlement in Argentina. It lasted two years before succumbing to an attack by native peoples.

Despite the early reports and expectations, large deposits of silver were never discovered in Argentina. For many years, Spain and Portugal colonized more productive lands to the north, while Argentina remained relatively untouched. After the conquest of the Incas in Peru, the Spanish established the Viceroyalty of Peru with its capital at Lima, on the Pacific coast of South America. At its height in the seventeenth century, the viceroyalty (a territory whose leader is the representative of a monarch) would include all the Spanish-speaking colonies of South America with the exception of Venezuela.

Early explorers in Argentina hoped to discover a land filled with precious metals, jewels, and other riches. When they observed indigenous people wearing silver jewelry, they thought that the area must have vast reserves of the metal. Unfortunately, although Argentina has many other resources, silver is in short supply.

In 1536 Pedro de Mendoza established the settlement that would become Buenos Aires. This settlement was abandoned in 1541, and in 1573 the town of Córdoba was founded in the foothills of the Andes. Sitting astride the overland route to Lima, Córdoba served as the main gateway for Argentina's trade. The founding of Córdoba also marked the start of colonizing the Argentine interior, a long and difficult process.

Seeking a trade route to bring silver from Peru across the Andes to the mouth of the Río de la Plata, Spanish colonists built small settlements along the rivers of the Chaco region. These first Spanish settlements struggled for many years with river flooding, disease, and raids by the indigenous peoples. Although Argentina had fertile land for crops and livestock, the first colonists faced a labor shortage. The Guarani, Huarpe, Comechingon, and other indigenous peoples did not adapt well to forced work on Spanish plantations, and many died from overwork or disease. While a few river and coastal settlements endured, the Río de la Plata estuary was unsafe for settlement until 1580.

▶ The Viceroyalty

In 1580 a group of settlers from Asunción, the capital of what became Paraguay, returned to the shores of the Río de la Plata to rebuild

LAND OF DIVERSITY

The transatlantic slave trade brought hundreds of thousands of African slaves to Argentina and other South American countries between the 1500s and the 1700s. By the time slavery ended in Argentina in the mid-1800s, Buenos Aires had a large African American population. Some of these residents were freed slaves or the descendants of slaves, while others had immigrated voluntarily from Africa or other parts of the world.

Buenos Aires. Many of the people of Buenos Aires came from other Spanish colonies in South America, including Peru and Chile. The city traded its goods through the overland route to Peru. The first colonists built farms, raised crops, and tended herds of livestock in the surrounding countryside.

Despite the newly revived city of Buenos Aires, Spanish monarchs continued to neglect Argentina. The area remained a remote and undeveloped part of the Viceroyalty of Peru, and its merchants were not even allowed to trade directly with Spain. By law, Buenos Aires had to trade through the viceroyalty's capital of Lima, where the ministers of the viceroyalty had their customs and inspection stations. Outside of the cities, the region's native peoples fiercely resisted the influence of the newcomers. Colonists and settlers in

In the early 1700s, an indigenous group called the Araucanians fled Spanish settlement of their ancient homeland in Chile. They crossed the Andes to Argentina's pampas, where they tamed wild horses, traded with other groups, and eventually developed a settled agricultural life.

search of more land waged an ongoing war against Argentina's indigenous groups throughout the 1600s.

At this same time, the Catholic Church began sending Jesuit missionaries into Argentina's interior to build missions, hoping to convert the indigenous people to Christianity. Some of these missions would later form the nucleus of important Argentine frontier towns. The city of San Miguel de Tucumán, which had a strong trade economy, also developed into a religious and political capital of northern Argentina. Córdoba also became an important center of culture and higher learning.

In the late eighteenth century, the busy trade through the port of Buenos Aires and the threat of conflict between Spanish and Portuguese colonies prompted Spain to reorganize its South American possessions. In 1776 the Viceroyalty of the Río de la Plata was officially established with its capital at Buenos Aires. This colony included what became Argentina, Uruguay, Paraguay, and Bolivia. The Spanish government allowed the merchants of Buenos Aires to trade directly with the home country, a measure that brought an influx of new settlers from Europe.

◉ The Fight for Independence

Direct rule by a Spanish viceroy did not sit well with Argentina's colonists. Those who lived in the interior longed for independence and had already established a secondary capital at Córdoba. This town became the seat of the developing Argentine independence movement.

At the same time, the British saw a chance to gain colonies in South America. Spain was busy with war in Europe, and Britain hoped to take advantage of the opportunity. On June 27, 1806, British troops under General William Beresford captured Buenos Aires. But a revolt of the townspeople drove out the British troops, who retreated permanently from Argentina in 1807. These events became known as the Reconquista of 1806 and the Defensa of 1807. After their defeat, the British signed a treaty of peace with Santiago Liniers, the Spanish viceroy.

Like the Spanish, the British were also occupied with the situation in Europe. The ambitious French leader Napoleon Bonaparte had marched troops into Spain and had placed the country under the rule of his brother Joseph Bonaparte, unseating King Ferdinand VII. The Argentines saw their chance for independence. On May 25,

Napoleon Bonaparte

1810, a *cabildo,* or town council, unseated the viceroy and formed a new government in Buenos Aires. Ferdinand VII regained his throne in 1814, but by this time the Argentines were in open revolt against Spain.

On July 9, 1816, an official proclamation of independence at San Miguel de Tucumán led to the founding of the United Provinces of the Río de la Plata, a new state that included Argentina and other South American countries. In 1817 General José de San Martín invaded Chile through the Andes Mountains to attack Spanish forces. San Martín won a decisive victory against the Spanish in 1818, a battle that permanently drove Spanish troops from Argentina and marked the successful end of Argentina's revolution.

This **monument in Buenos Aires** commemorates General José de San Martín's historic battle, which won Argentina's independence from Spain.

The fight for independence had succeeded, but it had also brought deep divisions between different political and social factions within the United Provinces. Uruguay and Paraguay would leave the federation and establish separate republics. In Argentina, an urban faction centered in Buenos Aires and known as the *porteños*, or "people of the port," opposed the caudillos (powerful landholders with personal armies) who sought sovereignty for their rural towns, estates, and provinces. This division between the city and the country settled into a pattern in which political leaders generally sided with either the unitarios, who favored a strong central government, or the federales, who favored independence for the provinces.

In December 1824, delegates from throughout Argentina met in Buenos Aires to decide on the form of a new national government. In February 1826, the assembly elected Bernardino Rivadavia as the first president of the United Provinces of the Río de la Plata. However, many of the rural caudillos and farmers opposed both Rivadavia and the new constitution drafted by the assembly in Buenos Aires.

After independence, Rivadavia was eventually forced from power and the national government collapsed. A federale leader, Colonel Manuel Dorrego, took over, but Argentine officers opposed to Dorrego's decisions overthrew his government in 1828. Dorrego was executed in 1829, and General Juan Lavalle took power in Argentina.

◉ Political Turmoil

The coup that deposed Dorrego did not heal the bitter divisions within Argentina. Opposing General Lavalle was a charismatic federale leader, the wealthy landowner Juan Manuel de Rosas. A legislature dominated by the federales elected Rosas governor of Buenos Aires in 1829. Rosas had the support of provincial caudillos as well as the merchants of Buenos Aires. He was also

Juan Manuel de Rosas, governor of Buenos Aires from 1829 to 1832 and from 1835 to 1852, made his fortune as a cattle rancher.

helped by the members of a secret society known as the *mazorca*, which carried out the torture and execution of thousands of Rosas's political opponents, as well as of many native peoples who had continued to resist Argentine rule.

Rosas's tyrannical and violent government gained him many enemies. During the 1830s, an opposition party formed in Montevideo, the capital of Uruguay, among Argentine exiles. In the meantime, rebellion was also brewing in the countryside. General Justo José de Urquiza, the governor of Entre Ríos Province, joined the opposition against Rosas. Rosas fled Argentina for permanent exile in Britain, while Urquiza called for a constitutional convention to settle once and for all the framework of Argentina's government. Meeting in the town of Santa Fe, the delegates produced a new Argentine constitution modeled on that of the United States. The constitution established a confederation with Paraná as the first capital and Urquiza as the first elected president. Although the unitarios of Buenos Aires opposed this government, wanting Buenos Aires to be its own independent state, Urquiza marched troops into the port city and forced it into the confederation in 1859. The rivalry between Buenos Aires and the provinces would continue through the rest of the century.

In 1862, during the presidency of General Bartolomé Mitre, Buenos Aires became the nation's capital. Over the next few years, Mitre drew Argentina into the Triple Alliance, a military partnership with Brazil and Uruguay. In 1865, when Paraguayan dictator Francisco Solano López declared war on Brazil, Argentina refused to allow Paraguay's army to cross Argentine territory. Solano López then declared war on Argentina as well. By 1870 the Triple Alliance had won a complete victory against Paraguay.

▶ Immigration and Prosperity

Argentina's rich, untapped natural resources, and the peace that followed the victory of the Triple Alliance, attracted a wave of European immigrants. Spaniards, Italians, and Britons filled the booming port of Buenos Aires, while new railroads carried the newcomers inland to the fertile pampas and to the huge agricultural estates known as *estancias*. New farm machinery and the invention of barbed wire, as well as the building of irrigation canals, allowed the ranchers of the pampas to raise crops and livestock.

While these settlers made new lives in Argentina, some of the nation's original inhabitants faced growing challenges. By 1879, after many years of resistance, the last indigenous groups on Argentina's western frontier had been defeated by troops under General Julio Rocahad—a defeat that marked the end of a determined battle by

Covered wagons pulled by oxen transported trade goods and European immigrants across Argentina's pampas.

Argentina's settlers to wipe out nearly all of the land's native population. By the late 1870s, the number of indigenous Argentines, who had thrived before the region's colonization, had shrunk drastically.

Roca was elected president in 1880, and his government finally managed to settle the political status of Buenos Aires. In a compromise with the unitarios, who insisted on statehood, Roca's government established the city of Buenos Aires as a federal district. This district remained separate from the province of Buenos Aires, which had its own capital in the city of La Plata.

At this time, European countries in search of profitable foreign investments extended generous credit to Argentina while British engineers arrived to build a new transportation network. A railroad linked the two principal cities of Córdoba and Buenos Aires in 1880, allowing the fast shipment of grain and beef to the docks of the capital. Refrigerated ships carried these exports across the Atlantic, and Argentina's economy thrived from the sale of grain and beef.

The **railroad** linking Córdoba to the seaport at Buenos Aires sped up the sale of Argentine agricultural products on the world market.

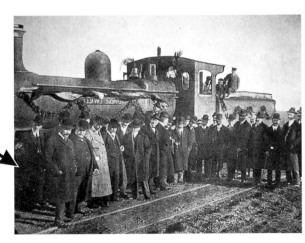

Rapid growth and heavy investment created problems as well as prosperity. As foreign money flooded into Argentina, and as the government spent its own money freely, the country experienced damaging inflation. Prices for ordinary goods and food skyrocketed, causing unrest among workers, many of whom saw little benefit from the economic growth despite their labor. The government's mismanagement of the nation's money spurred public suspicions of corruption. Discontent also festered in the Argentine military, which staged a revolt against the government. A series of leaders and the ongoing political turmoil brought the rapid rise of an opposition party known as the Unión Cívica Radical (Radical Civic Union, or UCR).

The continued unrest and accusations of corruption convinced President Roque Sáenz Peña, who took power in 1910, to pass an electoral reform that required all male adults to vote in a secret ballot. Prior to this reform, Argentina's leaders had entered office through military power or political influence—but not by a popular vote. In 1916 Hipólito Irigoyen, the UCR candidate, became the first Argentine president to be freely elected by the people. But the Argentine military, which firmly opposed the UCR, remained a strong presence. A series of violent strikes took place between 1916 and 1919, spurred by Argentina's still-struggling economy. This unrest convinced many conservative politicians to cast their lot with the army, which to many people seemed to be the nation's most stable institution. The situation only worsened in 1929, when a worldwide economic depression contributed to unemployment, hunger, and discontent within Argentina. In 1930 Irigoyen was overthrown by a military coup that established a

regime under General José Félix Uriburu. This government only lasted until 1932, when General Agustin Justo was elected. A series of military dictators followed throughout the 1930s.

Hipólito Irigoyen, Argentina's first elected president, doffs his hat to the crowd.

Meanwhile, events in Europe were also affecting Argentina. In 1939 Nazi Germany had attacked Poland, an event that touched off World War II between Germany's Axis alliance and the Allies, led by Great Britain and France. Argentina declared itself neutral, a policy opposed by groups who favored the Allies. The country grew increasingly unstable as the ruling party fought for control of the legislature as well as the streets. In 1943, after the death of General Justo, General Pedro Ramírez, the minister of war, overthrew President Ramon Castillo and established a military government.

The Era of Perón

Colonel Juan Domingo Perón, a military leader who had the support of Argentina's labor unions and workers, was elected president in 1946. In 1948 Perón and his followers established a political party called the Peronistas. Strongly nationalist, the party favored a centralized government, the rights of workers, and limited influence by the Catholic Church on education and public life. Perón's second wife, María Eva Duarte de Perón, nicknamed Evita, was extremely popular

Juan Domingo Perón, shown here as a lieutenant general, began his military career at age sixteen by attending Argentina's national military academy. Visit vgsbooks.com for links to additional information on Juan Perón and his second wife, Evita.

among Argentine families and workers. Evita's charisma helped Perón win
reelection in 1951.

Evita

Perón's policies transformed
Argentina. The government instituted
a system of benefits for workers,
reformed the education system, and
put Perón's supporters in control of
the judicial system and public administration. Nevertheless, Perón had
powerful opponents in the army as
well as in the Catholic Church, which
still enjoyed widespread support
among ordinary Argentines. Perón's
social policies, especially the legaliza-
tion of divorce, eroded his support among church leaders, while his
authoritarian regime drew the opposition of university students. His
popularity suffered further after Evita's death in 1952. In 1955 the
armed forces deposed Perón and forced him into exile in Spain. During
the late 1950s and 1960s, Argentina continued to seesaw between military and civilian governments.

By the late 1960s, Argentina was reeling from violent demonstrations against military dictatorship and a faltering economy.
Underground movements took to remote forests and mountain
foothills to carry out sabotage and kidnappings. In 1970 one such
group, known as the Montoneros, kidnapped and murdered former
president General Pedro Aramburu in order to stop his attempt to
return Argentina to constitutional government.

To end the chaos, many Argentines called for the return of
the charismatic Juan Perón. In March 1973, the Frente Justicialista
de Liberación, a coalition that included the Peronistas, won control
of Argentina's legislature. Soon afterward, Perón returned to
Argentina. In September he won a presidential election and named his
third wife, María Estela Martínez de Perón, nicknamed Isabelita, as
vice president.

Military Rule

At this time, the economy of Argentina was suffering from high debts,
high inflation, and rising unemployment. To combat these problems,
Perón's government passed tightly controlled government budgets—in
sharp contrast to Perón's earlier policy of generous public spending.
This effort squeezed workers who depended on benefits such as health
and unemployment insurance and pensions.

Perón died in July 1974 and was succeeded by his wife, who had little political experience. In the meantime, the ongoing economic problems sparked turmoil among Argentine workers, and strikes and demonstrations became commonplace. In March 1976, the military intervened to restore order. A three-man military junta (a ruling committee) took power, with General Jorge Videla, the army's commander in chief, serving as the president. The junta dissolved the legislature, banned strikes and political activity, and imprisoned thousands of its opponents. Argentines called this campaign La Guerra Sucia, or the "Dirty War," and called those who had been kidnapped and murdered by the government *los desaparecidos* ("the disappeared").

In March 1981, General Roberto Viola succeeded Videla as president. In December he resigned due to poor health and was replaced by Lieutenant General Leopoldo Galtieri, who pledged to return Argentina to a more liberal form of government. But Galtieri could not cope with the nation's crushing foreign debts or with high inflation, which was pushing working families deeper into poverty. The populace grew increasingly restless as it became apparent that the military leaders did not have the solution to the country's chronic economic crisis.

In April 1982, the armed forces decided to pursue a quick and decisive military victory in the hope of regaining public support. Argentina invaded the Islas Malvinas, or Falkland Islands, which had been under British rule since 1833. To combat the invasion, the British sent naval forces to the islands and reclaimed the islands in June. (A state of war between Argentina and Great Britain continued until the two countries agreed to a cease-fire in October of 1989.)

▶ Amnesty and Economics

The defeat in the Falklands forced Galtieri out of office and pressured other military leaders to resign from government service. Elections held in October 1983 brought the UCR to power and Dr. Raúl Alfonsín to the presidency. In response to public

MARCHING MOTHERS

In 1977 a group of Argentine women began assembling in the Plaza de Mayo in Buenos Aires each week to protest the imprisonment and disappearance of their children and husbands. The Madres de la Plaza de Mayo became a powerful symbol of the public's opposition to Argentina's military dictatorship. Even after the fall of the junta, they continue to meet regularly to honor the desaparecidos and remember the Dirty War.

outrage over the crimes committed during the Dirty War, Alfonsín promised to prosecute military officers who had been involved. Some high-ranking officers were tried and sentenced, but groups allied with the military supported amnesty (pardons) for many of the accused. For the next decade, the issue of trial or amnesty played a prominent role in Argentina's political life. The debate caused a simmering resentment among the population and unrest within the military, where opposing factions fought openly for dominance.

Carlos Saúl Menem, the head of a three-party alliance that included the Peronistas, won election as president in May 1989. While the amnesty debate began to settle, the Menem administration took steps to head off a looming economic disaster. To reduce its budget deficits, the government sold state-owned industries and ended wage indexing, which tied some workers' raises to the rate of inflation. These actions affected the living standards of millions of government employees. Demonstrations against the measures took place, and corruption scandals swirling around Menem's cabinet of ministers weakened his support.

The economic austerity measures did not end the economic crisis, but they did succeed in slowing it down. Menem won election to a second term in May 1995. Fernando de la Rúa, a member of the UCR and the mayor of Buenos Aires, succeeded Menem in 1999.

After de la Rúa's election, Argentina's gradual recovery ended abruptly. In 1999 an economic crisis struck neighboring Brazil, one of Argentina's most important trading partners. Argentina's exports—which were vital to its economy—plummeted, touching off another recession.

Argentina's government had been able to stave off bankruptcy with loans from the International Monetary Fund, or IMF. But as the Brazil crisis sent shock waves through South America, Argentina's economy continued to slide. Unemployment rose and living standards dropped throughout the country. Shantytowns formed on the outskirts of large cities. By the summer of 2001, huge foreign debts and the return of inflation had caused the Argentine currency and stock market to go into a steep decline.

As the government scrambled to hold the economy together, it enforced austerity measures that dramatically cut wages, pensions, and benefits. These drastic measures sparked strikes, public protests, and demonstrations that ended in violence. The upheaval forced President de la Rúa to resign in December 2001. De la Rúa was followed by a series of short-lived interim governments that tried to return order to the country. By January 2002, Eduardo Duhalde had taken office. In October 2002, Argentina was struggling to repay IMF loans, and it remains to be seen whether the Duhalde will be able to overcome the nation's serious economic problems.

In March 2002, **Argentine president Eduardo Duhalde** *(right)* and International Monetary Fund official Anoop Singh *(far left)* met at the Casa Rosada to discuss Argentina's economic crisis.

Government

The Argentine Republic is comprised of twenty-two provinces, the Federal District of Buenos Aires, and the National Territory of Tierra del Fuego. Constitutional reforms adopted in August 1994 reshaped the federal government, which had formerly followed the constitution of 1853. A bicameral Congreso (congress) includes a Chamber of Deputies, with 257 members elected for four-year terms, and a Senado (senate) of 72 members, three from each province and the two national territories, who serve six-year terms. Each province also has a governor and provincial legislature and has the right to administer its own justice and educational systems.

The new constitution allows the president a term of four years and one-time reelection. As the country's commander in chief, the president appoints senior military officers, as well as ambassadors and Supreme Court justices. The president also appoints a cabinet of ministers who are responsible for various national interests such as defense, justice, education, foreign affairs, labor, and social welfare.

The Supreme Court of Argentina, which decides issues of constitutional and national interest, includes nine justices, who must be appointed by the president and confirmed by a two-thirds vote of the senate. Federal courts of appeal in Buenos Aires and other major cities have jurisdiction over criminal, administrative, and civil matters. There are also supreme courts and lower courts of appeal in each province.

THE PEOPLE

More than any other modern Latin American society, Argentina is a product of European immigration and reflects the impact of European culture. At the start of the nineteenth century, the newly independent nation held large populations of indigenous people as well as African slaves and their descendants. As settlement spread to the south, west, and north of Buenos Aires, the indigenous peoples were pushed aside or absorbed into the general population. At the same time, a wave of new immigration from the European continent was taking place.

▶ Ethnic Heritage and Language

This great age of immigration to Argentina began in the mid-1800s and continued until the 1930s. About half of the immigrants who arrived in this period came from Italy, and a large percentage also came from Spain. Others left Great Britain, France, Denmark, Poland, Russia, Japan, or the Middle East for better opportunities in a pros-

pering country. Each of these groups contributed its knowledge and specialties to the economy. The British, for example, built railroads and factories, while Spanish and Italian winegrowers established the Argentine vineyards that have earned a global reputation.

In the early twenty-first century, more than three-quarters of Argentina's people descend from European colonists or immigrants. Although Spanish is their everyday language, a variety of dialects and accents survived the transatlantic voyage. The Spanish of Argentina absorbed many words from Italian, while scattered communities of Germans continued to speak their ancestral tongue as a second language. Basque, Gaelic, and Sicilian dialects have survived in Argentina, while Hebrew and Yiddish are heard in the Jewish community. The country's largest cities have their own particular accents. In Buenos Aires, local slang called *lunfardo* developed among immigrants who blended French, German, African, Italian, Spanish, and Portuguese words.

The rest of Argentina's population is made up of indigenous peoples, whose ancestors lived in the region long before the arrival of Europeans, and mestizos. Mestizos are people of mixed European and indigenous heritage. This population grows larger toward Argentina's frontiers with Chile, Bolivia, and Peru. While mestizos make up an important faction of rural laborers and farmers, they have also been a mobile group that has sought better opportunities in Argentina's cities. In Buenos Aires, mestizos make up a large class of manual laborers and factory workers who inhabit sprawling suburbs. The mix of mestizo and non-mestizo groups in the nation's cities has sparked competition and tension, a situation worsened by the country's struggling economy.

The largest surviving indigenous group is the Kollas, or Quechua, whose members live mainly in the northwest but also in Patagonia and in urban centers such as Buenos Aires. There are also smaller groups such as the Pilagá in the north, the Guarani of the Chaco region, and the Araucanians of western Patagonia. The numbers of

For Quechua weavers from the Andes, the process of weaving includes caring for the animals that provide wool or fleece, shearing them, spinning and dyeing the yarn, and finally weaving. The patterns they weave vary by region.

these groups are dwindling, and many of them are in danger of extinction. Indigenous people have also arrived in Argentine cities from Chile, Bolivia, and Paraguay.

Argentina is one of the most urbanized nations in the world, with about 90 percent of its people living in towns and cities. In general, urban families are smaller than rural families. Religious practice is more prevalent in the countryside, but the cities offer better health, education, and job opportunities. The porteños of Buenos Aires set themselves apart from the farmers and gauchos (cowboys) of the interior, and this separateness is further reflected in culture and in the long-standing political rivalry between the federales and the unitarios.

The Wichi people of northern Argentina and Bolivia make up one of the largest indigenous communities in southern South America. But life for this group is growing increasingly perilous. Their homeland in the Chaco region is undergoing desertification, as irrigation projects and drought rob the area of its vital water supply. Nearly all the animals that the Wichi once depended on—including deer, peccaries, armadillos, and iguanas—have disappeared. The Wichi also face discrimination from other ethnic groups and from the government.

By 2002 the population of Argentina had reached 36.5 million, making it the third largest nation in South America after Brazil and Colombia. The annual rate of population growth of 1.1 percent means that Argentina's population will double in about sixty-four years. Of all the South American countries, only Uruguay is growing more slowly.

Religion

Catholic missionaries have been present in Argentina for centuries, yet those indigenous groups that remained isolated from European civilization and Argentine cities have preserved their traditional customs and rites. In addition, many indigenous groups believe in the power of shamans to heal sickness or injury.

Nonetheless, Roman Catholicism remains the nation's dominant religion, and it has deeply influenced Argentine culture. Catholicism was the faith of the early Spanish colonists and also of most of the more recent immigrants from Europe, and about 90 percent of Argentina's people have been raised as Catholics. The church

The architecture of this **church in the northern province of Salta** shows Spanish influence on Argentine culture and religion.

continues to maintain a powerful authority over the daily life of ordinary people. Until 1994 the constitution required that the president of the country had to be a Catholic.

Argentina allows its people freedom of worship, although the constitution still directs the government to support and sustain the Catholic faith. The government provides the church with annual funding, which is directed through the Secretariat of Worship in the Office of the Presidency. Argentine students may ask for instruction in their faith, which by law must be provided to them at their school, whether it is public or private. The Roman Catholic Church also operates its own system of primary and secondary schools and universities.

Protestant beliefs also arrived with immigrants from Europe, and a wide variety of Protestant denominations, including Methodist, Lutheran, and Episcopalian, are represented in Argentina. More than half of the Protestants in the country belong to Pentecostal churches. Many descendants of British immigrants attend Anglican services. There are Eastern Orthodox and Muslim communities living in Argentina as well, many of them concentrated in Buenos Aires. On important national holidays, people and leaders of all faiths are invited to the Catedral Metropolitana in Buenos Aires for a special Mass, or Catholic service.

The Jewish population of Argentina has roots in sixteenth-century settlement and later immigration, as well as the post-World War II flight of Jews from the Holocaust and war-torn Europe. This relatively large community is based in Buenos Aires. Jewish citizens play a strong role in Argentine culture and politics, but they have also suffered violent anti-Semitism. Terrorist bombs exploded at the Israeli Embassy in Buenos Aires in 1992, and another explosion rocked a Jewish community center in 1994. In provincial cities, Jewish cemeteries have been vandalized. Argentina still grapples with anti-Semitism, despite a federal law passed in 1988 that makes it illegal to discriminate against anyone on the basis of race, nationality, gender, or religion.

ARRIVAL AND EXODUS

During World War II, a large influx of Jewish immigrants arrived in Argentina seeking to escape persecution in Europe. They joined an established community of Argentine Jews that had its roots in European settlement from the 1500s. However, their new home was not perfect. Anti-Semitic sentiments had emerged in the early 1900s, and attacks on Jews remained a problem. In addition, although Argentina had officially declared neutrality in the war, Perón's government sympathized with Germany's Nazi Party. After the war, many Nazi leaders fled to Argentina.

In the early twenty-first century, many Jews, some of whose families have lived in Argentina for generations, are preparing to leave Argentina. They believe that the worsening economy and social conditions will increase anti-Semitism. Seeking more security and better opportunities, they are leaving for other nations.

The Libertad in Buenos Aires is the oldest synagogue (Jewish place of worship) in Argentina.

Argentine **drugstores,** such as this one in San Carlos de Bariloche, fill prescriptions paid for by Argentina's national system of health insurance.

Health and Social Welfare

Argentina has a comprehensive system of public health facilities. Public hospitals and clinics treat most patients, and a national system of health insurance, to which all workers contribute, funds doctor visits, surgeries, hospital stays, treatment, and prescription drugs. The country has attained some of the best health standards on the continent. The economic crisis at the beginning of the twenty-first century has necessitated budget cuts and spending restraints that have placed the system under great strain. Nevertheless, in 2002 the rate of infant mortality—the number of infants who die before their first birthday—stood at 17.6 deaths per 1,000 live births, well below the South American average of 31. Life expectancy was 77 years for women and 70 years for men, several years higher than the averages for South America as a whole.

Argentina's extensive public health spending has largely eliminated communicable diseases such as smallpox and yellow fever. But health standards still vary throughout the country, especially between developed and rural areas. In addition, shantytowns that rise on the edges of the large cities, mostly built by immigrants from the countryside, often suffer outbreaks of disease caused by poor diet and sanitation.

Social welfare benefits include allowances for families, unemployment insurance, and a system of pensions for retirees, disabled people, and survivors (those who have lost a spouse through illness or injury).

For links to websites where you can learn more about the people of Argentina, including indigenous groups, and the problems they face, go to vgsbooks.com.

To pay these benefits, the government collects a percentage of each worker's paycheck and also levies taxes on employers.

The struggling economy has also affected the social welfare system, as the government makes cutbacks and tries to bring its budget into balance. In 1993 the government passed a law that set up a system of private pension funds, allowing workers to choose between private and public pensions. The debate over public spending has pitted those who favor keeping the traditional benefits against those who want to focus on balancing the budget and lowering public spending.

Education

Before the 1900s, Argentina suffered from a poor system of public education. Few children attended school, either private or public, and a large portion of society could not read or write—conditions that were also common in the rest of South America. Reform of the schools began in the early 1900s and took on special importance under the government of Juan Perón, when the state made large investments in education. The government offered new textbooks and a new curriculum, but the courses took on a political bent, and teachers were expected to instill support for the regime.

Students board a school bus in Rosario, Argentina, in 1955. During Perón's presidency in the 1950s, schools such as the Colegio Americano were pressured to teach respect for his government.

Beginning in the 1970s, Argentina's military government put a national reorganization process in place. Under this program, schools lost funding, the regime censored textbooks, and professors and scholars often found themselves in conflict with government policies. Demonstrations and resistance swept through the universities, many of which were forced to shut their doors. Professors and administrators who criticized or opposed the regime in power were often fired, and sometimes their universities were closed by the government. The result was a sharp decline in the quality and availability of higher education.

By the 1990s, schools and universities had begun to recover from the political turmoil of previous decades. Like the nation's other social institutions, the public school system was negatively affected by the economic and budget crises. However, Argentina still considers itself an education leader in Latin America. Argentines take pride in their country's university system, its scholarly journals and writers, and its five Nobel Prize winners.

A NOBEL HERITAGE

Argentina has had five Nobel Prize winners. Carlos Saavedra Lamas became the nation's first honoree when he won the 1936 Nobel Peace Prize for his work as a leader and diplomat in South America. Eleven years later, in 1947, the Nobel Prize in medicine went to Bernardo Alberto Houssay for his study of pituitary hormones. In 1970 Luis Federico Leloir was awarded the Nobel Prize in chemistry for his research of sugars and carbo-hydrates. In 1980 the human rights supporter Adolfo Pérez Esquivel became Argentina's second Nobel Peace Prize winner, and in 1984 César Milstein's study of the immune system made him the second Argentine to earn the Nobel Prize in medicine.

Bernardo Alberto Houssay, the son of immigrants from France, was seventeen when he graduated from the University of Buenos Aires. He is shown here as a Nobel Prize winner in 1947.

Buenos Aires students take a break from their studies to spend time with their friends.

The public education system in Argentina requires all children between the ages of six and fourteen to attend school. After completing primary school, about 67 percent of all students elect to continue their education. An ordinary secondary school diploma, the *bachillerato*, requires five years of study, while degrees in technical subjects usually take six years. There are more than eighty private and public universities in the country, as well as teacher colleges and specialized vocational institutes that prepare students for careers. The National University of Córdoba, which was founded in 1613 and officially gained university status in 1622, is the oldest institution of higher learning in the country. The University of Buenos Aires is the nation's largest.

Free and compulsory public education has brought the literacy rate within Argentina to more than 96 percent, one of the highest in Latin America. Yet illiteracy remains a serious problem in remote provinces such as Chaco, Corrientes, and Formosa, where many students attend school for only a few years. To combat illiteracy in rural areas, the government launched a national plan for literacy in 1985, a program that built thousands of small schools to teach reading and writing to adults.

Urban schools also have their share of problems, including a high dropout rate among poorer students, many of whom feel pressure to enter the workplace as soon as possible to support their families. To combat this trend, Argentina has begun the *jornada completa* (full-day) campaign, which will increase the average length of a school day from four hours to seven or eight hours in lower secondary schools (grades seven through nine). Educators hope that students will be less likely to drop out if they have more time with teachers.

CULTURAL LIFE

Traditionally, the cultural and artistic life of Argentina arose in two distinct societies: the Europeanized city of Buenos Aires, which many Argentines call the Paris of South America, and the rural nation of farmers, mestizos, indigenous peoples, and particularly gauchos. To Argentines, gauchos have always been heroic figures of solitary courage, strength, and self-sufficiency.

In their music, art, and literature, creative Argentines have identified themselves with one of these two opposing camps. To critics and students, the "classical" art and music of Argentina arrived with European influences, while the "folk" culture was homegrown but outside the mainstream. The porteño culture of Buenos Aires has historically dominated Argentina's cultural life, but in the mid-twentieth century new styles and forms imported from the countryside began to share the spotlight.

The clash and combination of the New World of South America and the Old World of Europe continue in the twenty-first century.

This dual nature lends a vitality to Argentine culture that shows up not only in works of art but also in the daily habits of work, family life, eating habits, and leisure time.

Holidays and Celebrations

The most important religious holidays in Argentina are Christmas and Easter. Argentine workers celebrate Labor Day on May 1, while May 25 marks the anniversary of the revolution in 1810, and Independence Day is July 9. The fight over the Falkland Islands brought about Malvinas Day on April 2, which marks the seizure of the islands by Argentina. On August 17, Argentines commemorate the death of General José de San Martín, the leader who defeated the Spanish and won Argentine independence. Columbus Day is traditionally celebrated on October 12, although a renamed mid-October "Day of the Americas" has begun to replace Columbus Day.

Many provinces of Argentina have their own celebrations to honor a patron saint or local hero. In the city of Salta, for example, pilgrims arrive between September 6 and September 15 to honor images of Jesus and the Virgin Mary. The relics washed ashore in Peru in 1592 and were carried from there to Salta. In the seventeenth century an earthquake suddenly ceased when they were paraded through town, and this event inspired the belief that the images protect the city from natural disasters.

Music

Argentina's musical traditions draw on the influences of European classical music, Spanish folk music, and the music and song of Argentina's indigenous people. The classical Argentine tradition began in the nineteenth century, when composers wrote many operas in the style of the Italian composers Gioacchino Antonio Rossini and Vincenzo Bellini. Composers Amancio Alcorta and Juan Pedro Esnaola lived and worked in Buenos Aires, where the Teatro Colón became a national center of performance. Alberto Williams, the founder of the Buenos Aires Conservatory, wrote orchestral and chamber music in the European style. Alberto Ginastera combined Argentina's folk styles with the harmonic innovations of twentieth-century European composers, producing many piano works that are known throughout the world. Argentine composers began to take up folk music in the 1900s. The songs and dances of the pampas and the gauchos were heard in *El Matrero,* an opera written by Felipe Boero and first performed in 1929.

The most famous musical product of Argentina is the tango, a passionate and bittersweet dance music. Musical historians still debate

This artistic tribute to the **tango** appears on the exterior wall of a building in La Boca, a district of Buenos Aires.

The popular Argentine singer **Carlos Gardel** collaborated in composing tango songs, including the two songs excerpted below at right. For the opportunity to learn more about tango artists and to listen to tango music, visit vgsbooks.com.

the origins of the tango, which by tradition began in the slums and portside nightclubs of Buenos Aires in the late nineteenth century. Tango enjoyed worldwide popularity in the early 1900s, and in the twenty-first century tango competitions still take place in dance halls all over the world. As music, tango is a broad category that includes three genres: instrumental, dance, and song music. Yet all tangos have one thing in common: the *bandoneón*, a type of accordion that was brought to Argentina from Europe in the 1800s. Among tango performers, the singer Carlos Gardel, who died in 1935, still holds the greatest renown among fans. After tango began to lose popularity in the 1950s, the composer Astor Piazzolla borrowed elements of American jazz to revive it in a style called *tango nuevo,* or "new tango."

Beginning in the 1930s, many folk music performers enjoyed national fame through recordings of their work. In the 1960s, the singer Héctor Roberto Chavero (also known as Atahualpa Yupanqui) arrived on the musical scene

TWO TO TANGO

The day that you love me there'll be nothing but harmony.
The dawn will be clear and the spring will be happy.
The breeze will quietly bring a rumor of melody.
And the fountains will give us their crystal song.

—lyrics from the tango "El Día Que Me Quieras (The Day You Love Me)" by Carlos Gardel and Alfredo Lepera; translated from the Spanish by Alberto Paz

My beloved Buenos Aires, the day I see you again, there will be no more sorrow or forgetfulness.

—lyrics from the tango "Mi Buenos Aires Querido (My Beloved Buenos Aires)" by Carlos Gardel and Alfredo Lepera; translated from the Spanish by Joseph Del Genio

Mercedes Sosa received a Latin Grammy in 2000 for best folk album for *Misa Criolla (Folk Mass).*

from Argentina's more rural provinces, performing many songs with a political message. Many Argentine musicians used folk music as a form of protest under repressive military governments. One of the most famous of these, singer Mercedes Sosa was a leader of the musical movement known as *nueva canción* ("new song"), a form of protest music that first arose during the Peronist regime. As folk music's popularity began to fade, *rock nacional* ("national rock") came to the forefront in the 1980s, drawing on heavy metal, country, reggae, tango, and Brazilian styles such as the bossa nova.

Outside of the cities, rural musicians took up the guitar and a drum known as the *bombo* and performed in different styles. The gauchos of the pampas have been almost as famous for their dancing as for their herding. The *chacarero, milonga,* and *malambo* are all famous gaucho dances. In the highlands of the northwest and west, indigenous musicians perform in a style known as *música andina,* or "Andean music," using drums, a ten-stringed guitar known as the *charango,* and many different kinds of reed flutes. The melodies of música andina are commonly sung in Quechua or Aymara, languages commonly spoken in the Andes region.

◉ Literature and Art

Argentine writing has its origins in the accounts of European travelers, including Ulrico Schmidel, Martín del Barco Centenera, and Ruy Díaz de Guzmán. The independence movement inspired Argentine writers of the early nineteenth century, and the revolution brought a new national literature into being. Authors Domingo Faustino Sarmiento and José Hernández led this new movement. The best-known work of Hernández, *El Gaucho Martín Fierro*, describes the struggle of a gaucho against the civilizing and often corrupting influences of the cities. The "gaucho novel" became one of the most popular forms in Argentine literature and continued in the twentieth century in the works of Benito Lynch and Ricardo Güiraldes.

Argentine writing and literary movements found an important outlet in the journal *Sur*, a magazine begun in the 1930s by the author and publisher Victoria Ocampo. *Sur* attempted to bridge the differences between European and native South American culture. For many Argentine writers, literature was a battle fought between competing styles, such as the realism of Manuel Gálvez and the surrealism of Adolfo Bioy Casares. Horacio Quiroga, an immigrant from Uruguay, wrote a short story collection called *Anaconda* that described the life and struggles of human beings in the natural wilderness.

Jorge Luis Borges, by contrast, was a writer of the city and a student of the hidden meanings of written language. In his poetry and stories, Borges wrote in a dense style and built complicated and intertwined plots. His mysterious and gripping tales won a worldwide audience, as did the novels of Manuel Puig, a writer fascinated by movies and other aspects of pop culture. Puig's first book was *Betrayed by Rita Hayworth*. He is best known for *Kiss of the Spider Woman (El Beso de la Mujer Araña)*, a novel that was transformed into a renowned play as well as a hit movie.

For the stage, Francisco Defilippis Novoa and Armando Discépolo wrote plays in a genre known as *grotesco criollo*, a tragicomic style that expressed the problems of rural immigrants arriving in the very different society of the city. Later in the twentieth century, political issues dominated the plays of Griselda Gambaro and Eduardo Pavlovsky. Two Buenos Aires theaters, the Teatro Abierto and Teatro de la Libertad, presented the works of these and other playwrights.

Argentina's film industry began in the 1930s, when the "tango film" became one of the country's leading cultural exports. Among the best-known Argentine movies of the pre-World War II era are *Prisoners of the Land* and *Such Is Life*. In the 1960s and 1970s, movies such as *The Hour of the Furnaces* and *Rebellious Patagonia* addressed political subjects. Some films of the 1990s, such as *The Face of the Angel*, have depicted events of the Dirty War.

Argentine artist **Claudia Bernardi** adds finishing touches to a mural.

Religion dominated Argentine art until the nineteenth century, when painters and sculptors adopted new themes such as exploration, settlement, and the Argentine revolution. Cándido López, a soldier severely wounded during the War of the Triple Alliance, painted canvases depicting many of the war's most important battles and events. Benito Quinquela Martín, a muralist, took up the harbors and shipyards of Buenos Aires as his theme. Scenes of rural life and the countryside inspired the paintings, drawings, and stories of Florencio Molina Campos. In the twentieth century, other Argentine artists took up many of the experimental styles pioneered in Europe. One of the best known, Alejandro Xul Solar, worked in the surrealist style. In the 1970s, pop art and conceptual art tested the knowledge of critics and the understanding of the public. Claudia Bernardi is a painter and a human-rights activist whose art is heavily influenced by the legacy of the Dirty War. Her work has been shown in galleries around the world and was part of a 2002 exhibit in Israel that focused on South America's twentieth-century dictatorships.

⦾ Sports

Argentines have been fans of soccer since British immigrants introduced it in the nineteenth century. The country has produced many international stars, including Gabriel Batistuta and Diego Maradona. The Argentine national team won the World Cup in 1978 and 1986. Cities and towns compete in several national leagues, with each team drawing the support of loyal—sometimes fanatical—followers.

Argentina has also produced stars in many other sports. Argentine race car drivers, including Juan Manuel Fangio and Carlos Reuterman, won many victories on the international Formula One racing circuit. In professional tennis, Gabriela Sabatini and Guillermo Vilas have both won top rankings. Angel Cabrera, a native of Córdoba, has gained international recognition on the professional golf circuit. Argentine national teams also compete in the British sports of rugby and cricket.

Argentines also love any sport or recreational activity connected with horses. Horse racing has millions of fans, and a society of owners and trainers have united to form a busy network of "jockey clubs."

Argentine soccer star **Diego Maradona** takes charge of the ball in a 2001 exhibition game.

Argentina has many fine equestrians and its polo players are among the best in the world. The gaucho sport of *pato* is an old game that still has its fans and players. In traditional pato, two teams on horseback compete over a leather pouch holding a pato (duck). In modern pato, the teams attempt to score goals using baskets at either end of a long field—a combination of polo, football, and basketball.

Argentines in search of good hiking travel to the Andes or Patagonia, which still have wild regions almost untouched by the outside world. Resorts in the high Andes attract skiers during the South American winters, while eco-trekking in Argentina's rain forests is popular with many international travelers.

Food

The pampas region, the breadbasket of Argentina, has been producing grain and cattle for more than a century, and inexpensive beef remains the staple in the diet of many Argentines. Per capita, Argentines are among the world's top beef eaters, and the barbecue *(asado)* remains a favorite social gathering for both urban and rural people. Beef is grilled, baked, stuffed into empanadas (beef pies), and mixed with corn and potatoes in a stew known as *locro*. The influence of Italian immigrants appears in the pasta and pizza dishes that have become national favorites. A wide variety of fruits and vegetables are grown and available at markets, and for refreshment many Argentines enjoy yerba maté, a refreshing herb tea grown in the north that is especially popular with rural workers and families. Maté is served in a small gourd (also called a maté) and is sipped through a thin reed or a silver straw called a *bombilla*.

The traditional main meal of an Argentine family takes place at midday, but work customs are changing eating habits. Many families eat a light breakfast and lunch, waiting until the late evening to enjoy the main meal of the day.

This Argentine enjoys sipping her yerba maté through a bombilla.

EMPANADAS

Argentine cooks usually fill these delicious pies with beef, but substitute potatoes, spinach, or other vegetables for a vegetarian version.

Dough:

2 cups all-purpose flour

1 teaspoon salt

½ cup water

6 tablespoons shortening

Filling:

2 tablespoons olive oil

1 onion, chopped

2 to 3 garlic cloves, minced

½ pound lean ground beef

1 tablespoon oregano

1 teaspoon paprika

1 teaspoon cumin

tomato sauce or
pasta sauce (optional)

½ cup green olives, chopped

½ cup raisins

1 hard-boiled egg, chopped

salt and white pepper to taste

sugar for sprinkling

1. Preheat oven to 400°F.
2. To make the dough, combine flour and salt. Add water and shortening and mix well.
3. Knead dough until smooth. Form into a cylinder and slice into 12 rounds.
4. In a large saucepan, heat oil and sauté onion and garlic until tender. Add ground beef and brown.
5. Stir in oregano, paprika, and cumin and continue to cook until beef is done. If the meat seems dry, add enough tomato or pasta sauce to moisten.
6. Mix in the olives, raisins, and egg and add salt and pepper to taste.
7. Roll out a circle of dough. Scoop about one tablespoon of the meat mixture onto the dough. Fold the round in half, forming a semicircle. Close the empanada by slightly moistening the edges with water and firmly pressing them together with the tines of a fork. Repeat with remaining filling and dough.
8. Brush the tops of the empanadas with a bit of water and sprinkle with sugar. Place on a cookie sheet and bake about 25 minutes, or until golden.

Serves 6 to 8

THE ECONOMY

For decades, the state of the economy has been the most pressing issue in Argentina's political and social life. Although the country was once the most prosperous in Latin America, political turmoil combined with foreign debts and the declining value of exports created chaos in the late 1970s and 1980s. Argentina suffered a round of hyperinflation in the 1980s, a time when the national currency swiftly lost value. Most working families saw their savings disappear and their lives grow increasingly difficult.

To control inflation and public debt, President Menem and the minister of the economy, Domingo Cavallo, implemented sweeping reforms in the early 1990s. To stop the fall in the value of the peso, Argentina's currency, it was linked to the U.S. dollar in a fixed exchange rate. This anti-inflation measure made the peso as strong as the U.S. currency on foreign exchange markets. To cure the nation's chronic budget deficits, Argentina also sold some of its government-owned companies and slashed its generous public spending, which had

gone toward salaries, social welfare benefits, education, and the public health system. The government also passed a series of decrees to reform its budget practices. Among other things, these decrees gave employers more leeway to fire and hire their employees, required that salary increases be tied to increases in productivity, and reduced the cost to employees of social security and other benefits.

At first, Cavallo's reforms and the new laws brought promising results. The linkage with the U.S. dollar controlled inflation and made outside investors more confident. The country's gross domestic product (GDP)—the total value of goods and services produced in Argentina—began to grow steadily. Between 1990 and 1994, Argentina's economic growth was second only to that of China.

At the same time, however, Argentine workers found their pay and benefits squeezed by the government's economic austerity measures. Salaries fell. Unemployment began to rise, as employers laid off thousands of workers. Workers who lost their jobs or who kept them at lower pay saw no improvement in their lives compared to the time of hyperinflation.

The mid- to late 1990s brought other serious problems from the outside. Debt crises in Mexico and Brazil worried foreign investors, who began pulling their money out of Argentina's banks and companies. As the country began to slip into recession, the labor unions called for protests of the austerity measures. Many Argentines saw the measures as unfair because outside lending agencies, such as the World Bank and the IMF, had insisted on them. By the summer of 2001, Argentina had reached a point of economic crisis. Interest rates soared, and the debt load again threatened national bankruptcy. Argentina's leaders took drastic action and froze savings accounts to prevent citizens from withdrawing their money from the banking system and sending it overseas.

The Mexican debt crisis of the 1990s inspired a catchy phrase among journalists: the Tequila Crisis. The collapsing Argentine economy of 2001 gave birth to a new headline: the Tango Crisis.

In December 2001, President de la Rúa resigned amid violent protests and demonstrations by Argentines who had lost faith in their government. A few days later, a new president, Adolfo Rodríguez Saa, announced that Argentina would stop making payments on $141 billion in foreign debts. Saa, lacking support from Argentina's political

Argentine workers protest IMF-mandated cuts in government spending for public schools and health care. They hold signs and banners facing the Casa Rosada in Buenos Aires where the national legislature meets.

parties, resigned in late December. In January 2002, Eduardo Duhalde took office and promptly stopped the one-to-one linkage of the peso to the dollar in the hopes that this would ease high interest rates and boost the country's exports. Meanwhile, throughout the crisis, Argentina's cities were shaken as angry citizens took to the streets. Protesters denounced the government and demanded relief from unemployment and poverty, while riots descended into violence and looting. Although the World Bank and the IMF sought to help Argentina overcome the crisis, in March 2002 approximately one-fifth of Argentines were without jobs. In September 2002, leaders warned that, without more aid, the country might not be able to pay its debts. Argentina stood on the brink of an economic collapse that could affect the rest of South America and the entire world economy.

> As Argentina's economic crisis reached its peak, the reigns of presidents and interim leaders lasted only days. Between December 20, 2001, and January 2, 2002, a total of five men held office.

Manufacturing

Despite its recent troubles, Argentina once had the strongest economy in South America. In the late nineteenth century, the huge export market for Argentine beef began an era of rapid industrialization. Companies built meatpacking plants, known as *frigoríficos*, in several cities, a move that brought new investment in a variety of related businesses such as milling, leather making, food processing, and the making of leather clothes and shoes. Although agriculture had long been Argentina's biggest business, manufacturing gained great importance in the early 1960s. The government established new steel, oil, and automobile factories, and smaller private companies turned out enough clothing, shoes, and other consumer goods to meet demand. Within ten years, the country was exporting large quantities of manufactured goods and recording a growing trade surplus, meaning Argentina was selling more of its goods abroad than it was buying from foreign countries.

But the country's growing economic problems, especially the hyperinflation of the 1980s, discouraged the foreign investment needed to develop new industries such as electronics and technology.

Visit vgsbooks.com for up-to-date information about Argentina's economy and a currency converter (according to the current exchange rate) that shows you how many pesos are in a U.S. dollar.

In addition, while the peso's link to the dollar made imported goods cheaper, it also raised the cost of production and made Argentina's manufactured exports less competitive on the world market.

By the beginning of the twenty-first century, Argentina's manufacturing was employing about 18 percent of the nation's workers and contributing about 20 percent to the GDP. The most important manufactured products were food and leather goods, steel, automobiles, refined oil, chemicals, textiles, and software. Argentina's strong and growing pharmaceutical and medical industries have benefited from investment by multinational firms as well as domestic companies such as Bagó and Roemmers. Textile companies draw on the country's wool and cotton production, and Argentina also produces cement, refined sugar, olive oil, and wine.

Farming and Forestry

The fertile and level landscape that dominates Argentina produces ample food for domestic consumption as well as for export. In the early twentieth century, even as Argentina industrialized, most of its business was linked to agriculture. Grain and cattle have long been the traditional staple products, while wheat remains the nation's single most important crop, taking up much of the available farmland in the pampas. Alongside wheat fields are acreages of corn, soybeans, and sorghum, which are raised for animal feed.

By the end of the 1990s, farming was employing about 10 percent of the labor force and providing 6 percent of the GDP. Beef cattle from the pampas are still the country's most valuable export. Sheep graze in the drier areas of the southern pampas and Patagonia.

Argentina's cattle ranches exported more than 230,000 tons (209,000 metric tons) of beef in 2002.

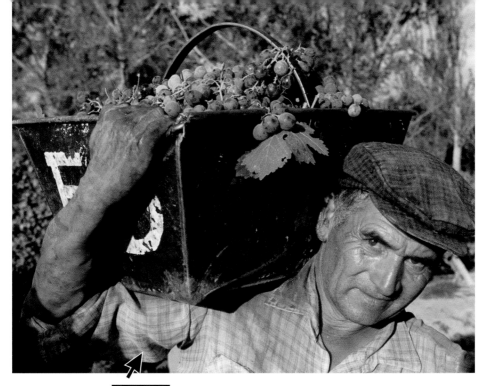

Many small **vineyards** had been established in Argentina by the end of the sixteenth century. In modern times, Argentina is the fifth largest wine producer in the world.

Argentina's successful wine industry is centered in the northwestern provinces of Mendoza and San Juan. In the northern provinces, grapes and a wide variety of other fruit crops are also grown, including apples, pears, and citrus trees that thrive in the subtropical climate of the Mesopotamia region. Irrigation projects around the Río Negro and other southern waterways have allowed farmers to plant productive fruit groves in parts of Patagonia. Argentine plantations produce yerba maté, made into a popular drink, as well as tea. Sugarcane is grown in Tucumán, Salta, and Jujuy Provinces, side by side with small tobacco farms.

The forestry industry produces sawed logs for construction and pulp for paper manufacturing, as well as firewood and charcoal. The quebracho of the Chaco region supplies tannin, a vital element of the leather-making process. Pine and cedar trees that grow at higher and drier elevations are used to make paper pulp, while the low-lying tropical forests of northern Argentina provide lumber for housing and furniture.

Cutting tropical hardwood trees has created an environmental problem of rapid soil erosion—a serious problem throughout Argentina, where flash floods and heavy rains have destroyed much of the land that the country depends on for farming.

In Argentina **power plants** are 60 percent thermal (burning coal, oil, or natural gas). Another 31 percent are hydropower plants that rechannel water to generate electricity, and the remaining 9 percent are nuclear.

Mining and Energy

Argentina's growing mining industry increased its contribution to exports throughout the end of the twentieth century. Large foreign investments, brought by the country's gradual economic recovery in the 1990s, helped the industry expand. These investments financed the exploration of remote regions where geologists suspected that reserves of minerals, oil, and natural gas might be present. By 2000 Argentine mining was generating about $1 billion a year and was exporting more than half of its production.

Argentina's mineral resources, although not as vast as its early colonists hoped, are enough to support a healthy mining industry. One of the nation's largest mines, El Aguilar, produces lead and zinc in Jujuy Province. Mines scattered throughout the nation supply iron ore, uranium, silver, copper, lead, and manganese. The new Bajo de la Alumbrera mine began operating in the late 1990s and extracts gold and copper ore.

Argentina has also benefited from plentiful resources of oil, natural gas, and other resources to become self-sufficient in power production. Southern Patagonia produces limited amounts of black and brown coal. The country's rivers have provided the raw energy for many hydropower projects. Deposits of crude oil lie off the shores of

Patagonia, supplying electricity generators as well as oil refineries that make gasoline and other fuels. Argentina also has abundant natural gas reserves in the northwest around the province of Salta. New projects are under way to develop gas pipelines from the Loma de la Lata field in Patagonia—the largest such field in Argentina. These lines would export gas to Chile and other South American countries.

Services

The service industry in Argentina grew rapidly during the 1980s and 1990s, as Argentina created a new economic sector in white-collar industries such as finance, insurance, banking, and retail trade. Services have surpassed traditional manufacturing in importance. The service sector employs more than half the workforce and contributes about half of the country's GDP.

Many of Argentina's service employees work in hotels, restaurants, and other businesses that serve visitors to the country. Tourism, particularly in Buenos Aires and in the wilderness regions of Patagonia, has brought income without requiring heavy capital investment. The nation's troubles in 2001 and 2002 may deter some visitors, but Argentine tourism experts hope that the drastic drop in local prices will attract budget-conscious travelers.

Foreign investments have been an important engine driving the service industry in Argentina. Carrefour, a French retailer, has opened retail stores in several Argentine cities, and several restaurant chains from the United States have created franchise networks in the country. Small-business franchising, in which store and restaurant owners buy the right to sell a branded service or product, was a popular way for people to run a business of their own until the dire economic crisis of 2001 made investment impossible for many Argentines.

Mercosur and Foreign Trade

In 1991 Argentina joined Brazil, Paraguay, and Uruguay in signing the Treaty of Asunción, an agreement that led to the creation of the Southern Common Market (Mercosur) in 1994. In 1996 Bolivia and Chile became associate members. Mercosur eliminated all tariffs on goods moving among participating countries, except for textiles, steel, automobiles, and petrochemicals, which remained under tariffs until 1999. In addition, the Mercosur countries settled on a common external tariff charged on goods imported from or exported to non-member countries. The Mercosur countries aim for a total common market by the year 2006. As part of this common market, all Mercosur members will have to coordinate their economic, environmental, and technology policies and allow goods and people to move more freely across their common borders.

Trade among the Mercosur countries increased dramatically after the agreement. Although the income from tariffs fell, the earnings from increased foreign trade have made up for the loss. Between 1993 and 1997, the value of Argentina's export trade with the Mercosur countries tripled from $3.7 billion to $9.5 billion. Until Brazil's economic crisis in 1999, about one-third of Argentina's exported goods were sold to this neighboring Mercosur member.

Foreign trade was the engine that drove Argentina's prosperity in the late 1800s and early 1900s. It continued to make up a vital economic activity in the late twentieth century, although the peso's link to the dollar tended to make Argentine products expensive for foreign buyers. Argentina suffered a trade deficit during the last part of the twentieth century, but the busy export trade to Mercosur has helped to compensate for deficits with North America and with the European Union, a common market of European nations.

Attending a 2001 **Mercosur meeting** in São Paulo, Brazil, Argentina's economy minister, Domingo Cavallo *(right)*, confers with his Brazilian colleague, Pedro Malan *(left)*.

In the late 1990s, Argentina's principal exports were machinery, crude oil, chemicals, and agricultural goods, including grain, beef, and animal feeds. Argentina imported vehicles, office machines (such as computers), paper products, and telecommunications equipment. With the recent turmoil putting the nation's economic future in jeopardy, Argentines hope that the country's strong record of profitable export will help the economy recover.

◉ The Future

Despite its economic problems, Argentina remains one of Latin America's most productive nations, with the highest gross national income (GNI) per capita in South America in 2001. Argentine products have been sold to foreign markets for more than a century, and the healthy trade surplus remains in place, a vital support for the domestic economy. Argentina has historically benefited from a comprehensive public health system, high literacy, and extensive natural resources. Until recently, the nation had finally been enjoying hard-won political stability after many years of turmoil.

Yet the country's future remains uncertain. Argentina veered on the brink of bankruptcy in early 2002, and the government still must cope with billions of dollars in foreign debt. This debt, combined with growing unemployment and rising prices, acts as a brake on economic growth, preventing new investment in industry and services. Lending institutions such as the IMF and the World Bank will extend credit only under certain conditions, a situation that may force Argentina's government to enact even tighter controls on public spending. The return of inflation and recession will also cause foreign investors to avoid Argentina in favor of the many alternatives in Latin America.

Solving economic problems takes not only sound government planning but also popular will, and Argentine workers are growing weary of the heavy sacrifices, in wages and benefits, demanded of them. Many Argentines resent the influence of foreign lenders and institutions on their country and have lost all confidence in their leaders. Calls for further austerity and cuts in public spending may, in turn, provoke continued public discontent. The country may even see a return to the struggle for power between civilian and military leadership that characterized late-twentieth-century Argentina. Whatever the future holds for Argentina in the twenty-first century, the nation will have to draw on the many strengths of its land and its people to succeed.

A.D. 1300s–1400s The Incan Empire controls regions north of what would become Argentina.

1516 The Spanish navigator Juan Díaz de Solís sails up the Río de la Plata.

1520 Ferdinand Magellan explores the Río de la Plata, Argentina's Atlantic coast, and what would become the Strait of Magellan.

1526 Sebastian Cabot establishes Sancti Spiritus, the first European settlement in Argentina.

1536 Buenos Aires is founded by Pedro de Mendoza.

1541 Settlers abandon Buenos Aires and move to Asunción (in what became Paraguay).

1580 Juan de Garay reestablishes Buenos Aires.

1613 National University of Córdoba is founded.

1776 Spain establishes the Viceroyalty of the Río de la Plata, with Buenos Aires as the capital.

1806–1807 The British invade Buenos Aires but soon withdraw after a counterattack.

1810 A revolutionary government is set up in Buenos Aires, marking the start of the fight for Argentine independence.

1816 An assembly at San Miguel de Tucumán declares an independent nation, the United Provinces of the Río de la Plata.

1826 A constituent assembly establishes a presidency and elects Bernardino Rivadavia as the first president of the United Provinces.

1843 Argentine forces blockade Montevideo, Uruguay.

1852 General Justo José de Urquiza defeats Argentine dictator Juan Manuel de Rosas at the Battle of Caseros.

1853 A new constitution is adopted, a new capital is founded at Paraná, and General Urquiza is elected president.

1859 Urquiza incorporates Buenos Aires into the new constitutional framework, unifying the nation.

1865–1870 Argentina joins forces with Brazil and Uruguay to defeat Paraguay in the War of the Triple Alliance.

1879 The Argentine military concludes a long war against indigenous people in the north and west.

1890–1900	Argentina endures an economic crisis, giving rise to opposition groups such as the Radical Civic Union (UCR).
1912	A reform of the election law requires all male citizens to vote.
1930	The military overthrows President Hipólito Irigoyen, ending seventy-seven years of constitutional government.
1936	Carlos Saavedra Lamas becomes the first Argentine to win a Nobel Prize.
1939–1945	World War II
1946	Colonel Juan Perón wins the presidency by election.
1955	General Eduardo Lonardi leads the overthrow of Juan Perón.
1969	Riots and demonstrations, known as the Cordobazo, take place in the provinces.
1973	The Frente Justicialista de Liberación political coalition wins a majority in the legislature. In October Juan Perón is reelected as president.
1974	Juan Perón dies and his widow, María Estela Martínez de Perón (Isabelita), inherits the presidency.
1976	Military officers overthrow President Martínez de Perón's government, and a three-man military junta takes power.
1978	Argentina wins its first World Cup in soccer.
1982	On April 2, Argentine troops land in the Falkland Islands. British forces retake the islands on June 14, leading to the resignation of Lieutenant General Leopoldo Galtieri.
1983	Dr. Raúl Alfonsín is elected president, and civilian government is restored.
1991	The currency reform of Domingo Cavallo pegs the Argentine peso to the U.S. dollar.
1994	A Jewish community center in Buenos Aires is bombed, killing eighty-six people.
2001	Argentina defaults on its foreign debt, sparking an economic crisis.
2002	Representatives of the International Monetary Fund (IMF) visit Argentina to discuss an economic recovery plan.

Fast Facts

COUNTRY NAME República Argentina (Argentine Republic)

AREA 1,073,512 square miles (2,780,400 sq. km)

MAIN LANDFORMS Andes Mountains, tropical forests, pampas plains, Valdés Peninsula, Tierra del Fuego

HIGHEST POINT Cerro Aconcagua, 22,834 feet (6,960 m) above sea level

LOWEST POINT Valdés Peninsula, 131 feet (40 m) below sea level

MAJOR RIVERS Río de la Plata, Río Colorado, Río Negro, Río Paraná, Río Salado

ANIMALS Swamp deer, peccaries, monkeys, capybaras, penguins, guanacos, jaguars, porcupines, armadillos, wild horses, alpacas, whales, pumas, foxes, hares

CAPITAL CITY Buenos Aires

OTHER MAJOR CITIES Córdoba, Rosario, Mendoza, San Miguel de Tucumán, Mar del Plata, Salta, San Justo, Ushuaia

OFFICIAL LANGUAGE Spanish

MONETARY UNIT Peso. 100 centavos = 1 peso.

Currency

ARGENTINE CURRENCY

The Argentine currency is the peso, which is divided into 100 centavos. Peso notes come in denominations of 100, 50, 20, 10, 5, and 2. Coins are in denominations of 1 peso and 50, 25, 10, 5, and 1 centavos. The U.S. dollar is also accepted as legal tender in

Argentina, and Argentine leaders are considering dollarization, which would make the dollar the country's official currency.

The Argentine flag consists of a horizontal white band between two light blue bands. This design was conceived during the nation's war of independence by General Manuel Belgrano at the site of modern Rosario. According to legend, Belgrano got the inspiration on the shores of the Río Paraná, while he was staring at the sky just before a battle. The flag was officially adopted in 1816 with the creation of the United Provinces. Centered upon the white panel is the Sun of May, an emblem added in 1818, with thirty-two alternating straight and wavy gold rays. Argentines celebrate Flag Day on June 20, the anniversary of Belgrano's death.

The lyrics of the "Himno Nacional Argentino," or the Argentine national anthem, were written in 1811 by Vicente López y Planes to celebrate the defense of Buenos Aires against the British. The melody was composed by J. Blas Parera, and in 1813 the song was adopted as the national anthem. An English translation of the anthem's first verse follows:

Mortals! Hear the sacred cry:
Freedom! Freedom! Freedom!
Hear the noise of broken chains.
See noble Equality enthroned.
The United Provinces of the South
Have now displayed their worthy throne.
And the free peoples of the world reply:
We salute the great people of Argentina!

For a link where you can listen to Argentina's national anthem, "Himno Nacional Argentino," go to vgsbooks.com.

MARTHA ARGERICH (b. 1941) A classical pianist born in Buenos Aires, Argerich launched her career with first prizes won at piano competitions in Bolzano, Italy, and Geneva, Switzerland, at the age of sixteen. She won the prestigious Chopin Competition in Warsaw, Poland, in 1965. She has recorded the music of Bach, Beethoven, Schumann, Liszt, Debussy, Ravel, and Bartók, and she plays at music festivals around the world.

JORGE LUIS BORGES (1899–1986) Argentina's most famous author of essays, poems, and short stories, Borges was born in Buenos Aires and moved to Europe with his family when he was fifteen. After World War I (1914–1918), he returned to Argentina and, in 1923, published *Fervor de Buenos Aires,* his first collection of poetry. He worked as an editor for *Sur,* Argentina's leading literary journal, and wrote a collection of short stories, *Ficciones, 1935–1944,* that gained worldwide renown. He won the National Prize for literature in 1956 and worked as a professor of literature at Buenos Aires University and as director of Argentina's national library.

ADOLFO PÉREZ ESQUIVEL (b. 1931) An architect, professor, and human rights leader, Esquivel left his job teaching architecture in 1974 to form Servicio Paz y Justicia, an organization of Latin American nonviolence groups. Esquivel lobbied for a permanent United Nations human rights commission. In 1977 he was jailed for his public criticisms of Argentina's military government. He was released the next year and was awarded the Nobel Peace Prize in 1980.

DIEGO MARADONA (b. 1960) Argentina's most popular soccer star, Maradona is considered by many to be the best player since the Brazilian star Pelé. Maradona achieved world fame as captain and most valuable player of Argentina's 1986 national team, which won the World Cup. He led the Italian Napoli team to Italian League championships in 1987 and 1990 and to a European Cup championship in 1989. Maradona officially retired from soccer in 1997.

JUAN PERÓN (1895–1974) Born in Lobos, Perón was a popular and fast-rising military officer. In 1943 he joined the plot to overthrow the civilian government of Argentina, and he gradually gained influence in the new military government. In February 1946, he was elected president. Perón favored policies of industrialization, public works to reduce unemployment, and state-supported public services and benefits for workers. Inflation, censorship, and corruption scandals plagued Perón's regime, and he was overthrown in 1955. In June 1973, he was reelected as president, but his term was cut short by his death in 1974.

MARÍA EVA DUARTE DE PERÓN (1919–1952) "Evita" was born in a small town near Los Toldos. She was an Argentine film and stage star who became the nation's First Lady in 1946 when her husband Juan Perón was elected president. An active political leader, she played a key role in convincing workers and labor unions to support the authoritarian Perón. Through the Eva Perón Foundation, she was responsible for the construction of new schools, hospitals, and a network of support institutions for the poor. She also fought for political and social equality for Argentine women.

ASTOR PIAZZOLLA (1921–1992) Born in Mar del Plata, Piazzolla was a classically trained musician who revived the tango and brought it to a worldwide audience. He was hired as a teenager by tango singer Carlos Gardel to play in the film *El Día Que Me Quieras (The Day You Love Me)*. He achieved national fame performing on the bandoneón, an accordion-like instrument featured in tango music. In 1960 he formed the Quinteto Tango Nuevo (New Tango Quintet), which performed in the jazzlike tango nuevo style that Piazzolla pioneered.

JUAN MANUEL DE ROSAS (1793–1877) Rosas, a native of Buenos Aires, supported the British invasion of Argentina in 1806–1807. After Argentina gained its independence, he fought for the federale faction against the unitarios. Rosas was the governor of Buenos Aires Province from 1829 until 1832 and again from 1835 until 1852. He used spies and assassins belonging to a network known as the mazorca to enforce a ruthless dictatorship from Buenos Aires. He was overthrown in 1852 and fled to exile in Britain, where he lived until his death.

GABRIELA SABATINI (b. 1970) Sabatini, whom many fans simply call Gaby, was born in Buenos Aires. She got her first tennis racket when she was six years old, and by the age of fourteen she was playing professionally. She competed in tournaments around the globe, winning the U.S. Open in 1990. She was South America's top-ranked player from 1985 until her retirement in 1996.

JUSTO JOSÉ DE URQUIZA (1801–1870) Urquiza, born in Entre Ríos Province, was the president of the Argentine confederation from 1854 to 1860. In the late 1850s, rebellion in Buenos Aires flared into war. Urquiza's defeat of Bartolomé Mitre, the leader of the rebels, reunited Argentina until 1861, when another conflict broke out. This time, Mitre was victorious, forcing Urquiza to retire. He was assassinated in 1870.

LA BOCA According to local tradition and some music historians, this Buenos Aires neighborhood was the birthplace of tango music. In the late twentieth century, it was transformed into a trendy quarter of brightly painted artists' homes and studios.

CAMPO DEL CIELO This natural site is in northern Argentina. Its name means "field of the sky," and it is famous for the ancient meteorite fragments that litter the ground.

CEMENTERIO DE LA RECOLETA This famous and very exclusive cemetery in Buenos Aires holds the elaborate memorials and tombs of some of Argentina's elite figures, including that of Evita.

CRISTO REDENTOR Visitors to this towering stone monument, also known as the Christ of the Andes, get a spectacular view. Built at an elevation of 13,123 feet (4,000 m) in the Andes Mountains, the statue commemorates the peaceful establishment of the border between Argentina and Chile.

ESTEROS DEL IBERÁ This lake and marsh region in northeastern Argentina provides a refuge for rare birds, reptiles, mammals, and the capybara, the world's largest rodent.

PERITO MORENO GLACIER This huge glacier in southern Patagonia attracts sightseers who hope to witness "calving," or the breaking off of immense towers of ice into Lago Argentino.

SALTA This old colonial city features an old cathedral, town hall, museum, and a train stop along the "Train to the Clouds," a line that climbs to the high elevations of the puna region.

SAN ANTONIO DE ARECO This former frontier town lies west of Buenos Aires in the heart of Argentina's cowboy country and is home to a gaucho museum and a rowdy gaucho festival every November.

TALAMPAYA CANYON The Talampaya Canyon in La Rioja Province is famous for bizarre rock formations and petroglyphs (prehistoric rock carvings).

VALDÉS PENINSULA Lying along the Atlantic coast, the Valdés Peninsula has been designated a natural reserve and is home to sea lions, elephant seals, and penguins.

desaparecidos: "the disappeared," meaning those who were arrested and executed by Argentina's military dictatorships of the 1970s and 1980s

estancia: a rural estate established in the early nineteenth century for cattle and horse ranching. Estancias were usually owned by the descendants of Spanish and other European settlers.

federale: in Argentine history, a person who favored the autonomy of provincial cities (specifically the power of local voters to elect their provincial governors), in opposition to the unitarios, who favored the centralized power of Buenos Aires

gaucho: a cowboy hired by the owner of an estancia to herd livestock and round up wild horses and cattle on the plains of the pampas

gross domestic product (GDP): the total value of all goods and services produced within a single nation. Similar measurements are **gross national product (GNP),** the total value of all economic activities carried out by the citizens of a single nation (regardless of where they are living), and **gross national income (GNI),** the total value of production within a nation plus income to the country from the rest of the world.

hyperinflation: a drastic fall in the value of currency, an event that usually forces prices to rise much more rapidly than wages

International Monetary Fund (IMF): an organization that extends loans, credit, and other economic support to developing nations

junta: a ruling committee whose members are drawn from the military

Perónist: a member of an Argentine political group that favored the policies of Juan Perón

porteños: "people of the port," meaning the people of Buenos Aires and its surrounding region

unitario: in Argentine history, a person who favored a strong central government under the authority of the capital of Buenos Aires (specifically, the power of the central government to appoint provincial governors)

Glossary

Selected Bibliography

***The Europa World Year Book 2001.* London: Europa Publications Limited, 2001.**
This annual publication covers Argentina's recent history, economy, and government, as well as providing a wealth of statistics on population, employment, trade, and more. A short directory of offices and organizations is also included.

Feitlowitz, Marguerite. *A Lexicon of Terror: Argentina and the Legacies of Torture.* New York: Oxford University Press, 1998.
After conducting hundreds of interviews with survivors, the author summarizes the effect on Argentina of years of terror by Argentina's military dictatorship during the Dirty War.

Foreign Area Studies, The American University. *Argentina: A Country Study.* Ed. James D. Rudolph. Washington, D.C.: U.S. Government Printing Office, 1986.
This volume in the U.S. government's **Area Handbook** series offers a comprehensive account of Argentine history and culture.

France, Miranda. *Bad Times in Buenos Aires: A Writer's Adventures in Argentina.* Hopewell, NJ: Ecco Press, 1999.
A British writer describes a climate of disappointment and failure in the streets of Buenos Aires, once the wealthy and glittering Paris of South America.

Fraser, Nicholas. *Evita: The Real Life of Eva Perón.* New York: W. W. Norton & Company, 1996.
This updated account of the life, works, and motivations of Eva Perón has become the standard biography of the most popular public figure in the country's history.

Hawthorn, Vic. *Argentina, Uruguay and Paraguay: A Travel Survival Kit.* Berkeley, CA: Lonely Planet Publications, 1992.
This book provides a very detailed travelers' guide to the Río de la Plata republics.

"Population Reference Bureau 2001 World Population Data Sheet," *Population Reference Bureau (PRB),* 2001, <http://www.prb.org> (April 12, 2002).
This annual statistics sheet provides a wealth of data on Argentina's population, birth and death rates, fertility rate, infant mortality rate, and other useful demographic information.

Rock, David, ed. *Argentina in the Twentieth Century.* Pittsburgh: University of Pittsburgh Press, 1975.
This book collects essays on the political and economic conditions within Argentina in the late twentieth century.

Shumway, Nicolas. *The Invention of Argentina.* Berkeley, CA: University of California Press, 1993.
A writer examines the history of Argentina through the literary themes that occur in the works of its leading poets, novelists, politicians, and philosophers.

Thornton, Richard C. *The Falklands Sting: Reagan, Thatcher, and Argentina's Bomb.* Washington, D.C.: Brassey's, 1998.
The author gives an account of the international diplomatic maneuvering during the Falkland Islands crisis, which ended with Argentina's defeat at the hands of a British naval force.

Turner, Barry, ed. *The Statesman's Yearbook: The Politics, Cultures, and Economies of the World, 2002.* New York: Macmillan Press, 2001.
This resource provides concise information on Argentine history, climate, government, economy, and culture, including relevant statistics.

Argentina Tour
Website: <http://www.argentour.com>
This fun site offers videos, music, maps, and more to acquaint the visitor with Argentina.

Borges, Jorge Luis. *Labyrinths: Selected Stories and Other Writings.* New York: W. W. Norton and Company, 1988.
Originally published in 1962, this collection is an introduction to the fiction and nonfiction writings of Borges, whom many rank as one of the leading authors of the twentieth century.

Chatwin, Bruce. *In Patagonia.* New York: Penguin, 1988.
The author takes a literary and poetic journey to the wilderness of Patagonia, describing miners, Charles Darwin, and a log cabin built by Butch Cassidy.

Collier, Simon, et. al. *Tango! The Dance, the Song, the Story.* New York: Thames and Hudson, 1995.
This colorful title offers a fun and informative glimpse into the culture and history of the tango, Argentina's national music and dance.

Dell'Oro, Suzanne Paul. *Argentina.* Minneapolis: Carolrhoda Books, 1998.
This book takes readers on a fun tour of Argentina, exploring its land, history, and culture.

Eagen, James. *The Aymara of South America.* Minneapolis: Lerner Publications Company, 2002.
This book discusses the history and culture of the Aymara, an indigenous group living in Argentina and other South American countries.

Parnell, Helga. *Cooking the South American Way.* Minneapolis: Lerner Publications Company, 2003.
This cultural cookbook presents recipes for a variety of authentic and traditional South American dishes, including special foods for holidays and festivals.

Partnoy, Alicia. *The Little School: Tales of Disappearance and Survival in Argentina.* San Francisco: Cleis Press, 1998.
This first-person account of an Argentine political prisoner was written by one of the few to have survived arrest and interrogation at the hands of Argentina's military dictatorship of the 1970s and 1980s.

Perón, Eva. *In My Own Words: Evita.* New York: The New Press, 1996.
In this English translation of *My Message,* Evita defends the economic and social changes brought about in Argentina by Perónism and the actions of her husband, President Juan Perón.

Rock, David. *Argentina, 1516–1987: From Spanish Colonization to Alfonsín.* Berkeley, CA: University of California Press, 1989.
This book provides a convenient and succinct summary of Argentina's history, covering political, economic, and social issues up to the late 1980s.

Further Reading and Websites

Shaw, Edward, and Reto Guntli. *At Home in Buenos Aires.* **New York: Abbeville Press, 1999.**
The authors create a photographic tour through the streets and homes of Buenos Aires, as well as a tour of the historic estancias of the countryside.

Southernmost South
Website: <http://www.surdelsur.com/indexingles.html>
This website, available in Spanish or English, offers a wealth of information on many aspects of Argentine life.

vgsbooks.com
Website: <http://www.vgsbooks.com>
Visit vgsbooks.com, the homepage of the Visual Geography Series®. You can get linked to all sorts of useful on-line information, including geographical, historical, demographic, cultural, and economic websites. The vgsbooks.com site is a great resource for late-breaking news and statistics.

Index

agriculture, 11, 19, 21, 28, 59, 60–61, 65
Andes Mountains, 4, 8, 9, 11, 13, 15, 16, 18, 23, 54, 68. *See also* Cerro Aconcagua
animals. *See* flora and fauna
Argentina: boundaries, location, and size, 4, 8, 16, 68; currency, 7, 34, 56–57, 59, 60, 64, 68; flag, 69; map, 6, 10; national anthem, 69; regions, 9–13, 54, 61
art, 46, 51–52
authors, 50–51

Boca, La, 17, 48, 72
Bolivia, 8, 9, 20, 25, 38, 39, 63
Bonaparte, Joseph, 25
Bonaparte, Napoleon, 25
Borges, Jorge Luis, 51, 70
Brazil, 8, 16, 28, 34, 58, 63, 64
Buenos Aires, 5, 17–18, 23, 24, 25, 26, 27, 28, 29, 33, 35, 37, 38, 39, 40, 41, 46, 48–49, 52, 63, 68, 69

Cabot, Sebastian, 22–23
Catholic Church. *See* religion
cattle and livestock, 5, 9, 11, 13, 14, 23, 24, 27, 28, 29, 54, 64, 59, 60
caudillos, 27
Cerro Aconcagua, 11, 68. *See also* Andes Mountains
Chile, 8, 12, 20, 26, 38, 39, 63
cities, 17–19, 24, 34, 37, 38, 39, 50. *See also* Buenos Aires; Córdoba; Rosario; Ushuaia.
climate, 15
Córdoba, 18–19, 23, 25, 29, 53, 68
Cristo Redentor, 11, 72
currency, 7, 34, 56–57, 59, 60, 64, 68

dance, 48–49
desaparecidos, los (the disappeared), 33
Díaz de Solís, Juan, 22
domestic challenges, 5, 7, 34, 41, 42, 45, 58–59, 63, 65
Dorrego, Manuel, 27
Duhalde, Eduardo, 34, 35, 59

economy, 5, 7, 29, 30, 32, 33, 34, 38, 41, 43, 56, 59–65

education, 31, 32, 35, 39, 40, 43–45, 57
energy, 15, 62–63
environment, 13, 61
Esquivel, Adolfo Pérez, 44, 70
estancias, 28
Evita. *See* María Eva Duarte de Perón

Falkland Islands, 8, 33
farming. *See* agriculture
federales, 5, 27, 39
flora and fauna, 9, 11, 13–14, 16, 21, 39, 54, 60–61, 68
food, 54–55
foreign trade, 24, 25, 29, 56, 59, 63–65. *See also* Mercosur
forestry, 61
forests, 4, 13, 61

gauchos, 46, 50, 51, 54
government structure, 35
Guerra Sucia, La (the Dirty War), 33–34, 51, 52

health, 39, 42, 57, 65
history: arrival of Europeans, 4, 15, 18, 22–23, 38; constitution, 27, 28, 35, 40; dictatorships, 5, 28, 30; fight for independence, 25–27; political instability, 7, 27–28, 30–31, 32–34, 56, 58–59, 65; World War II, 31, 40, 41
holidays and celebrations, 47–48
Houssay, Bernardo Alberto, 44

Iguazú Falls, 9, 16
immigrants, 4, 5, 17, 18, 28–29, 36–37, 39, 40, 41, 54
Incan Empire, 20, 23, 66
indigenous people, 12, 16, 20–21, 22, 23, 24–25, 29, 36, 38–39, 46, 48. *See also* mestizos
industry, 5, 15, 19, 34, 59–60, 65
inflation, 7, 30, 32, 33, 34, 56, 57–58, 65
International Monetary Fund (IMF), 34, 35, 58, 59, 65
Irigoyen, Hipólito, 30
Justo, Agustin, 30, 31

language, 37, 50, 68
Lavalle, Juan, 27
Leloir, Luis Federico, 44
literature, 46, 50–51

Madres de la Plaza de Mayo, 33
Magellan, Ferdinand, 22
manufacturing. *See* industry
maps, 6, 10
Maradona, Diego, 53, 70
mazorca, 27–28
Mendoza, Pedro de, 23
Mercosur, 63–65. *See also* foreign
    trade
mestizos, 38, 46. *See also* indigenous
    people
Milstein, César, 44
mining, 62–63
Mitre, Bartolomé, 28
Montoneros, 32
music, 46, 48–50
musical instruments, 49, 50

national anthem, 69
natural resources, 5, 15–16, 22, 23,
    28, 61, 62, 63, 65
Nobel Prize, 44

oil. *See* energy

pampas, 11, 13, 14, 15, 16, 17, 28,
    54, 60, 68
Paraguay, 8, 9, 16, 23, 25, 27, 28, 63
Patagonia, 12, 14, 15, 16, 17, 21, 38,
    54, 60, 61, 62–63
Peña, Roque Sáenz, 30
Perón, Juan Domingo, 7, 31–33, 41,
    43, 70
Perón, María Eva Duarte de (Evita),
    7, 17, 31, 32, 70
Perónistas, 31, 34
Piazzolla, Astor, 49, 71
plants. *See* flora and fauna
population, 17, 18, 19, 38–39
porteños, 27, 29, 46

rain forests, 4, 9, 54, 68
religion, 17, 25, 31, 32, 39–41, 52
Río de la Plata, 8, 16, 17, 19, 22, 23
Rivadavia, Bernardino, 27

rivers, 9, 12, 16–17, 19, 22, 23, 61,
    68. *See also* Río de la Plata
Roca, Julio, 29
Rosario, 19, 68, 69
Rosas, Juan Manuel de, 27–28, 71

Saavedra Lamas, Carlos, 44
Sancti Spiritus, 23
San Martín, José de, 26, 47
services, 63, 65
slavery, 24
soccer, 53
social welfare, 42–43
South America, 4, 7, 8, 20, 22, 23,
    24, 25, 34, 42, 43, 51, 65
sports, 53–54

tango. See dance
Tango Crisis. See economy
Tierra del Fuego, 8, 12, 14, 19, 22,
    35, 68
tourism, 63
transportation, 11, 29; Pan-American
    Highway, 11
Triple Alliance, 28, 52

Unión Cívica Radical (UCR), 30, 33,
    34
unitarios, 5, 27, 28, 29, 39
Uriburu, José Félix, 30
Urquiza, Justo José de, 28, 71
Uruguay, 8, 16, 25, 27, 28, 39, 63
Ushuaia, 19, 68

Valdés Peninsula, 12, 68, 72
viceroyalty, 23–25
Videla, Jorge, 33

writers. *See* authors

yerba maté, 16, 54, 61

Captions for photos appearing on cover and chapter openers:

Cover: Horses graze in the foothills of the Andes Mountains.

pp. 4–5 Flowers bloom along the Plaza de Mayo in central Buenos Aires.

pp. 8–9 Lake Nahuel Huapí is one of many Andean gems in Nahuel Huapí National Park in western Argentina.

pp. 20–21 More than 890 painted human handprints are preserved in the Cueva de las Manos (Cave of the Hands) in Patagonia, a region in southern Argentina. These paintings are 9,500 to 13,000 years old.

pp. 36–37 Buenos Aires schoolgirls gather for a snapshot with their classmates.

pp. 46–47 Gauchos, heroes in rural Argentine culture, drive cattle across the pampas of Patagonia.

pp. 56–57 As night falls, the portside pace in Buenos Aires slows.

Photo Acknowledgments

The images in this book are used with the permission of: © Trip/T Bognar, p. 4–5; © Robert Fried, pp. 8–9, 17, 26, 41, 45, 48; © Trip/D Ikenberry, p. 11; © Trip/N & J Wiseman, p. 12; © Trip/B Gadsby, p. 13; © Minneapolis Public Library, p. 14 (top); © Wolfgang Kaehler, pp. 14 (bottom), 42; © Michelle Burgess, p. 16; © Hubert Stadler/CORBIS, pp. 18, 20–21; © Trip/Eric Smith, p. 19; Historic Urban Plans, Inc., p. 22 (top); Library of Congress (LC-USZ62-30424), p. 22 (bottom); © Historical Picture Archive/CORBIS, p. 24; © Musée du Louvre, Paris/SuperStock, p. 25; © Robert Levine, pp. 27, 29 (bottom), 30, 32; © North Wind Pictures, p. 29 (top); Independent Picture Service, p. 31; © AFP/CORBIS, pp. 35, 53; © Trip/A Tovy, pp. 36–37, 58; © Jeremy Horner/Corbis, p. 38; © Trip/A Gasson, p. 40; © Three Lions/Hulton|Archive, p. 43; © Keystone/Hulton|Archive, p. 44; © Kit Houghton/CORBIS, p. 46–47; © Bettmann/CORBIS, p. 49; © Reuters NewMedia Inc./CORBIS, pp. 50, 64; © Veleria Galliso/courtesy of Claudia Bernardi, p. 52; © Trip/M Barlow, pp. 54, 60; © Stefan Poulin/SuperStock, p. 56–57; © Pablo Corral Vega/CORBIS, p. 61; © Trip/N Ray, p. 62; © Larry Luxnor, p. 68.

Cover Photo: © John Warden/SuperStock